Also by Jonathan Smith

Fiction
Wilfred and Eileen
The English Lover
In Flight
Come Back
Summer in February
Night Windows

Good Enough? (with Chris Cowdrey)
The Learning Game

The Following Game

Jonathan Smith

Peridot Press

First Published 2011

This Edition Published 2013

by Peridot Press,
12 Deben Mill Business Centre, Old Maltings Approach,
Melton, Woodbridge, Suffolk IP12 1BL
Tel: 01394 389850 Fax: 01394 386893
Email: enquiries@peridot.co.uk
Website: www.peridot.co.uk

ISBN: 978 1 908 095 69 5
eISBN: 978 1 908 095 14 5

Set and designed by
Peridot Press

Printed and bound in Great Britain
by Ashford Colour Press

I was a nuisance, tripping, falling,
Yapping always. But today
It is my father who keeps stumbling
Behind me, and will not go away.

Follower by Seamus Heaney.

Follow the fellow who follows the dream

Song, *Look to the Rainbow*

Jonathan Smith was, for many years, Head of English at Tonbridge School. As well as his acclaimed memoir, *The Learning Game*, which was described by Matthew Parris as 'the only book I have read on teaching which is not boring', he has published six novels and written many plays for radio. A film of his novel *Summer in February*, for which he wrote the screenplay, will be released in 2013. Jonathan is the father of the writer, Ed Smith, who played cricket for Kent, Middlesex and England.

for my brother David

Acknowledgements

I would like to thank David Kendall for the photograph on the front cover; my wife Gillie for the photograph on the back cover; and my daughter Becky for helping me to shape the book.

Derek Bingham, Jonathan Evans, Alex Sharratt, Scott James, indeed all at Peridot Press, have been a pleasure to work with; and I am particularly grateful to my excellent editor, Wendy Bosberry-Scott.

Finally, reading a book as personal as this is not always the easiest thing for those close to you, so a special thank you to Ed and my family for their support and understanding.

****

The following poems and extracts have been included with the kind permission of the authors and their publishers: Seamus Heaney: extract from *Follower*, in the collection *Death of a Naturalist* (Faber and Faber); R S Thomas: *Don't Ask Me*, from *Collected Later Poems 1988-2000* (Bloodaxe Books, 2004); R S Thomas: *The Bright Field*, from *Collected Poems* (1945-90) Phoenix Press (Orion Books); Tom Stoppard: extract from *The Real Thing* (Faber and Faber); Alun Lewis: *Goodbye*, from *Collected Alun Lewis*, Seren Books; *Acquainted with the Night* from 'The Poetry of Robert Frost', edited by Edward Connery Latham and published by Jonathan Cape, reprinted by permission of The Random House Group Ltd; Elizabeth Jennings: *Sensitivity*, from *Collected Poems*, Carcanet Press; the estate of Vernon Scannell for permission to use *The Loving Game*, from *Collected Poems*; and thanks to Vikram Seth for permission to use *Round and Round*, and *All You Who Sleep Tonight*.

Every effort has been made to locate and contact the publishers and/or copyright holders for materials reprinted in this book.

CONTENTS

2006

1.	JANUARY 2006	3
2.	DEPENDENCY	5
3.	J P R WILLIAMS	8
4.	A BIT OF LAST MINUTE SHOPPING	12
5.	GOOD HALL	14
6.	AGASSI, FATHER AND SON	19
7.	A GOOD GLARE	24
8.	HAD HE HIS HURTS BEFORE?	28
9.	BA FLIGHT 143	32
10.	DON'T ASK ME	38
11.	A ONE FOOTED BOY	41
12.	ROUND AND ROUND	48
13.	HORN PLEAS	49
14.	WATCHING TOM	52
15.	CORIOLANUS	55
16.	NOT WATCHING ED	60
17.	SO, JONATHAN, WHAT EXACTLY DID YOU TEACH ME?	67
18.	THERE IS NO GOD	71
19.	THE CAPTAIN WHO COULDN'T LOOK	73
20.	JOHN INVERARITY	82
21.	TEA WITH A LEDGE	89
22.	DOWN TO THE LAST BALL	93
23.	BELIEVING	97
24.	SUPERSTITION	105
25.	BATS	112
26.	ACQUAINTED WITH THE NIGHT	116

27. THE TABLES TURNED 121

28. WALKING 123

29. AS THE TEAM'S HEAD-BRASS 131

30. PESSIMISM 133

31. A GOOD DAY FOR A PESSIMIST 137

32. TO AN ATHLETE DYING YOUNG 141

33. A PASSAGE TO INDIA 142

34. A FATHER AT LORD'S 149

35. R E JONES, POET 153

36. YEARS BACK... 156

37. THREE IN THE MORNING COURAGE 157

38. IS HE GOING TO MAKE IT? 160

39. HEADS AND CAPTAINS 164

40. TALENT AND A BIT OF STEEL 167

41. SENSITIVITY 172

42. A COW JAM 177

43. ENJOY THE GOOD DAYS 182

44. THE BRIGHT FIELD 187

45. TRENT BRIDGE 188

46. AN INDIAN ALPHABET 196

2009

47. SAM IN THE STADIUM 201

48. INFLUENCES 205

49. THE LOVING GAME 213

50. LORD'S, 12TH JUNE 2008 214

51. IN A GARDEN IN ATHENS 217

PART ONE

2006

PART ONE

2005

1

January 2006

Today I put the novel I am writing on hold because there is something else, something more pressing, that I want to explore. It has been in the back of my mind niggling away for far too long, and for all that time I have been using every kind of ploy to deny its urgency, even to deny its importance. But I now know that it is my priority.

I want, if I can, to capture what it has been like to be a follower and a fan, but also to capture what it has been like to be a follower and a fan who happens to be the father of a professional sportsman who also happens to be a writer himself.

This was a book I was going to leave until after Ed Smith, my son, had retired. It had seemed better – more seemly and more sensible – to wait until he had hung up his boots, whenever that day came. It had seemed more balanced and mature to wait. Waiting for that day would surely afford us both a bit of distance, a proper perspective, and as a project this book would certainly be less risky because there would then be fewer hostages to fortune.

And yet I had planned to leave coming to terms with my life in teaching until after I had retired from the classroom, only to change my mind at the last moment and to write *The Learning Game* while I was still at my desk, still at the chalk-face, and still feeling the teacher's everyday rough and tumble. It is in a similar spirit that I want now to write about being a follower and a father while Ed is still playing, while it still thrills and still hurts.

The other reason I have decided to put my novel away for a while is that I was told last week that I have cancer. It's all right, don't worry, this is not going to be a book about cancer. There are plenty of those already. No, I just want to write this one because… well, obviously, because just in case… but more importantly because it feels the right moment to do so, and because when I think of doing so it feels fun. The idea has stopped coughing apologetically in the doctor's waiting room and, without bothering to knock, has barged straight into the surgery.

I will not tell anyone, least of all Ed, what I am up to. As is usual with me there is a touch of evasion involved in this strategy because he would, I suspect, try to dissuade me from this course. He would try to persuade me to go on with the novel. But after the surgeon had spelt things out to me and my wife in a clear matter of fact way and after the attendant nurse had given us a pile of what-you-need-to-know-about-your-condition leaflets, Gillie and I went, undefended, into a side consulting room to do the family phone calls.

First we rang our daughter Becky (who was feeding her newborn son) and then we rang Ed. He drove down straightaway from London to Kent and as he walked in the front door I knew I would start this.

Next week, as luck would have it – and the timing could hardly be better – Ed and I are off to India together. We are going on a trip, the trip of a lifetime, driving right across Rajasthan. From Delhi to Agra, then Jaipur, Udaipur, Jodhpur and on to Mumbai. He has set it up. He has been to India many times to play cricket and this time he has asked me along.

It will be my first visit. And it may be a little disloyal of me but while he thinks I am jotting down my impressions of temples or forts or my first sighting of a vulture, I will, on the sly, be up to something else, something a bit personal. Well, to cover my tracks, I will probably be doing a bit of both: a bit of looking out and a bit of looking in.

2

Dependency

This shadow, this dependency thing, goes back a long way with me. It unravels back to my early childhood. Not of course that I thought about it back then in such terms, but I did start circling around the issues in the mid-1950s.

In fact, I can be much more specific than that. I was reading a magazine and I was sitting on a train on my way to Brecon, on a train pulling slowly out of Newport station. I was fifteen or so – so this is probably 1957 – and I was reading an article written by Cecil Day-Lewis, the father of the actor Daniel Day-Lewis and later, in 1968, to be appointed the Poet Laureate.

This would have been *The New Statesman* I was reading, a journal I bought each week to make me feel an intellectual, or was it *The Listener*, anyway, in whichever it was Cecil Day-Lewis admitted, if that is the right word, confessed perhaps, to being a hero worshipper.

I can't find those sentences now but I do remember the sentiments: I can recall exactly the lines on which Cecil Day-Lewis was thinking. He confessed that he had always believed that some human beings were greater than he was – greater, finer, more talented, more gifted, *better* than he was – and that he hated the way that many modern people tried to increase their own importance by cutting everyone else down to their own puny size.

Yes!

I read his words again.

Yes!

I unscrewed my fountain pen (a Platignum, I hadn't got round to ball points) and wrote *Yes!* in the margin because (i) I was at the age when I saw the sight of my approval in the margin as a sign of scholarship and (ii) I did not want the distinguished men and women I followed, my heroes, to be downsized.

The whole point was that my heroes could do things that I could not, and I wanted my literary and sporting heroes to *be* heroes, not people like me. I not only admired their lofty presence, I needed their company every day of my life. Was the fifteen year old boy on that Welsh train inadequate, then, in some way? I am sure he was, very inadequate. And fifty years later he still feels the same way.

But hero-worshipping now sounds off-puttingly old-fashioned if not dead in the water. These days people are more likely to agree with Andy Warhol: 'You can only see an aura on people you don't know very well, or don't know at all.' The very concept of hero-worship feels out of date. It smacks of veneration. It smacks of homo-eroticism, of high-flown bright-eyed undeveloped youth, of Ancient Greece and Rome, of same sex crushes and recommendations for combat medals, a world altogether closer to the colossal than the life size, a world where rap is not a form of music but something small and administered across the knuckles.

I cannot fix the moment or date the day when hero-worship of my favourite sportsmen slid into hero-worship of my favourite writers. But sometime in my teens it did, and Thomas Hardy led the way. For many of my generation Thomas Hardy, rather than cannabis, was the gateway drug. His tragic tales were the dangerous first steps which led you on to a lifelong addiction to the hard stuff.

But no, 'slid into' is wrong. I didn't slide at all. It wasn't so much that I graduated from sport to literature or matured or anything ghastly like that, it was more that I just added writers to my list without deleting any of the players. As the weeks passed I was unconsciously arming myself with the insights of my heroic playwrights and my heroic poets and my heroic novelists. After reading Hardy I was no longer a boy but a man seeing the world with new eyes. In my letters and conversations (thanks to Jane Austen and Oscar Wilde and Samuel Butler) I was developing quite a nice line in what I liked to see as cool irony and subtle understatement, while deep down I was also being knocked sideways by Shakespeare and George Eliot and being blown away by Ibsen and Wordsworth.

It was as if I was not only seeing the world in a sharper way but seeing *through* it, seeing it for what it really was.

So when, on that day in 1957, I got back to school in Brecon I cut out and stuck the cautionary words of Cecil Day-Lewis inside the front cover of my grey ring binder essay file. And each time I sat down and opened the file I would see the quotation before I wrote my next critical essay (and my critical essays were very critical, stropping the edge of my blade until it was keen), essays on Addison or Emily Dickinson or Dryden or Marlowe or Pope or Swift or Vaughan, but the truth is that long before I got round to reading and writing about that march-past of literary heroes, I had attached myself to (*ie* had started to follow in a very obsessive way) the Great Tom Graveney, the England batsman, as well as the Great Welsh rugby teams and, as this was 1957, the Great Elvis Presley.

In fact, lying next to me on the train seat, and next up after I had finished reading *The New Statesman*, was a magazine full of Elvis Presley photographs, black and white photos of The King (with sultry eye shadow) singing *I Want You, I Need You, I Love You* and *Love Me Tender* in front of his ecstatic and adoring fans.

Even if I could not get my hairstyle to swoop and flick and settle in quite the same way as Elvis I was one of those adoring fans, an addict, an *aficionado*.

3

J P R Williams

Heathrow, flight BA 143 to Delhi.

We've checked our bags in and we will soon be called to board at Gate Number 14. While we wait we are in the Est Bar and having a mozzarella and tomato roll. It is while we are in there that I know the trip is off to the best of all possible starts because sitting a few feet away from us and drinking a pint of bitter is the greatest rugby fullback of his generation, J P R Williams.

No, it's lager he is drinking, not bitter. If you see a hero in the flesh and blood, Jonathan, particularly a Welsh hero, you might at least get the basic details right.

Wow.

JPR!

Right.

Yes, that is him, no doubt about it.

Tick.

Nerves kick in.

But straight away I have a problem. Do I speak to him? Do I tell him to his face what I consider his greatest performances were, what his absolutely finest moments were? I could describe them all and celebrate them all and given time I could place them in order of greatness from one to ten except where would I start? There are so many. Ten wouldn't do it. No, I'll just stand up, move one step and go for it:

-JPR, isn't it? Sorry to interrupt, you won't know me, but I just wanted to say that I have been watching rugby for over fifty years now and you were without any shadow of a doubt the greatest fullback of your or any generation-

As I am considering this approach the greatest fullback of his or any generation catches my eye and his eye says 'no'. It is a direct, no-messing look, and no one was better at direct no-messing than J P R Williams.

Fair enough, so I won't say anything. I let a few seconds pass and then I tap Ed's arm. He is sitting opposite me reading a newspaper, and I whisper,

-Ed.

-What?

-J P R Williams.

-Where?

My eyes flick right. Ed's eyes flick left. He very slightly nods, a barely perceptible reaction, and goes on reading. He is more used to sitting close to sporting legends. But Ed loves Welsh rugby as much as I do and will be excited because it is not any old sporting legend sitting there with his pint of lager, it is JPR.

Over the last twenty years we have spent countless hours sitting together on the sofa in front of the television assessing the strengths and weaknesses of the Welsh team, game by game, position by position, player by player, move by move, and above all encouraging them to be individual, to be Welsh in fact, and sometimes standing up and screaming at them to run, to run like the little genius Shane Williams runs, to trust in their instincts and to believe in their flair, which basically and usually means encouraging them not to play like the English.

J P R Williams.

He is smaller than I expected.

Let's think, he must be in his late fifties now.

JPR, full back, fearless, frightening, inspiring, fifty five caps, leonine, socks down, sideburns, brave under the high ball, devastating in defence, powerful in counter attack, unequalled in will, runs through a wall and asks 'Wall? What wall? Was there a wall there?' Six Triple Crowns, three Grand Slams, played ten times against England and never once on the losing side, and was fullback in the Lions teams that beat New Zealand and South Africa.

And, if you really want just one fearless frightening and inspiring example: in 1978, having had his face stamped on by an All Black boot he left the field in Bridgend and was stitched up by his father, a doctor, in the changing room before running back out to play on.

When I say he is smaller than I expected I mean he is less big. No surprises there, heroes often are. Even though I had been told he was small, Don Bradman was even smaller than I thought he would be, much smaller, with small hands. But JPR is still compact, still strong, his cheek is still scarred, of course it is still scarred, if some big New Zealand farmer stamps on your cheek with a big Kiwi rugby boot it's more than a scratch it's a scar for life, but JPR's cheekbones are prominent, no sign of middle age fat, and even though he is sitting down at the moment I can sense he has a very low centre of gravity.

I mustn't stare.

I look away.

I look back.

The pint glass is drained.

JPR has gone.

There is foam on the inside rim of his empty glass, and I am relieved I didn't go and make a fool of myself. On most occasions I am pathologically keen not to make a fool of myself as I very nearly did on the Eurostar coming back from Paris a few years ago when I was sitting opposite a woman who was reading one of my books. Now this rarely happens to me. In fact this happens so rarely to me that the whole thing was exquisite pain. I tried to look cool. I pretended to be absorbed in my own reading. Then I looked up and tried to appear arrested by something in the passing countryside, gosh isn't Northern France flat, but inside my jacket I was fingering my biro for the autograph (an autograph on the title page is even better than a tick in the margin) and my heart was off and running like Shane Williams and I was non-stop desperate for her to look up and look down at her book (at *my* book!) and open the back flap and look up and look down and double check and flush a bit and say,

-My God, no, I don't believe this, no, you couldn't be the author, could you?

I catch her eye. I am open to an approach.

-Sorry, did you speak?

-I just wanted to ask you if you're the author of-

She points at the book. With a modest shrug, a modest shrug practised so often that it comes very naturally to me, I say,

-Well, yes, I suppose I am.

But she never did ask, and it's not surprising she didn't as I hadn't allowed any photograph of myself on the dust jacket. No, that's not true. The truth is the publishers did not even ask me to provide one let alone go to the lengths of offering to pay for a photographer to drive down to my place in Kent. Such expensive things, photographs, Jonathan, and times are very difficult in the publishing business and we are looking at ways of cutting our costs, especially on books like yours.

On the credit side, though, she did keep reading that book of mine, so I did not fall at the first fence, and she kept on turning the pages, and 'a real page turner' is exactly the kind of review I like to have on one of my covers, it's much better than any old photograph, and she even popped a sweet into her mouth (and a very nice mouth it was) without taking her eyes off the book, which is the kind of readerly absorption I absolutely approve of.

4

A bit of last minute shopping

Just before our flight is called – BA Flight 143 to Delhi – Ed stands up and says he is off to buy a few things. I would never do anything as mad and as stressful as go last minute shopping when any flight I am booked on is about to be called. I ask him not to cut it too fine. He smiles at me and tells me to relax. And how exactly can I relax when he might be too late for the flight? *'This is the last call for Mr Edward Smith on flight 143. The gate is now closing.'* I do not want to be on my own in Delhi. I do not want to be on my own in Rajasthan. Right now I don't want to be on my own anywhere at all and though I have not told him this I nearly pulled out of this whole India trip in the morning because I had a panic attack when I was shaving.

He is back soon enough, though, and holding out a pair of trainers for me. He thinks the shoes I have on will not be all that comfortable as we walk the streets and sightsee all over India.

-You are size eleven, aren't you?

While he was away I took the chance to check that I have my passport and my ticket. I have. And have I got the poems? A few nights ago he asked me on the phone to bring along some of my favourite poems, and make sure they're short he said, just a few that you particularly like, your Desert Island poems, so that we can read and discuss them.

This request surprised me. Even though I have spent a lifetime 'teaching' poems and plays and short stories and novels, or 'appreciating' them, or 'criticising' them, or hoping I was helping my pupils to enjoy and to appreciate and to understand them, I have never been asked anything along these lines by my son. So I've slipped a selection in the same folder as my passport and ticket, which means that as I check my passport and ticket I am also aware of the poems. Yes, they're all still there, and they will travel well, these poems.

That's a relief.

Mental note: whatever happens, when I talk about the poems I must not sound like a teacher.

After seeing that I've got my passport and my ticket and the poems I do the even more shameful check (in the other side pocket of my shoulder bag) and this is to see that I have got my Malarone (for malaria), avoid being bitten and if symptoms persist see your doctor and if you feel dizzy do not drive, as well as my Immodium (can stop severe diarrhoea in one dose, that must take some doing) and my blackcurrant flavoured Dioralyte (fast and effective) for replacing lost fluids and body salts. The nurse at my GP's said it is very important in hot countries to avoid dehydration.

Thinking of surgeons, I've just remembered that J P R Williams is a surgeon. He is a surgeon somewhere in South Wales. Yes, in Bridgend, I think. I wonder what kind of surgeon he is? Might he be orthopaedic? Yes, that's it, I recall reading somewhere that he is an orthopaedic surgeon.

Bones and joints.

And if he is it makes sense. First of all JPR crash tackles his patients on the pitch, which cripples most of them, then he picks them up and slings them over his shoulder and carries them off to the operating theatre where he puts them together again on the slab, all in a day's work.

Anyway, an orthopaedic surgeon is not quite what I'll be needing, that's not quite my problem area.

-Are you all right, Dad?

-Fine, fine.

He puts his arm round me.

-You sure?

-Sure. And thanks for the trainers.

5

Good hall

It did not matter if it was sunny or raining or even getting dark outside. Twelve months of the year, whatever the weather, I would roll or throw or bowl tennis balls or cricket balls at Ed. It might be out in the back garden or along the runner carpet in the hall or up against the garage door or in the nets or in a squash court, and he would drill them back at me.

Drill is the word. Once – fortunately it was only a tennis ball – he drilled one back right between my eyes. I didn't see it coming or I reacted too slowly. That apparently was funny.

And when I wasn't being the bowling machine as well as all the fielders, Gillie or Becky were. Ed didn't really mind who bowled at him – his father, his mother, or his sister – as long as their arms were tireless and the balls kept coming, as long as we all put in the required hours.

If he hit the ball directly back at me, gunbarrel straight along the narrow runner carpet in the hall, it was 'Peter May' or 'Greg Chappell' or 'Martin Crowe'. This was in honour of three of the master batsmen known for playing straight, three great players noted for showing the full face of the bat to the bowler. Or, if he hit the ball straight back at me and we were being a bit less legend, it was simply 'good'. If the ball touched either wall in the hall, however, it was 'bad'. 'Bad' because he had hit 'across it' to the leg side or he was playing the shot 'inside out' to the off. And we didn't want that.

In later years, when I arrived at a county ground and peered at the pitch to find Ed was batting (rather than the last man out for, say, 7) and then saw one of his straight drives just to the left or just to the right of the bowler's stumps, with mid-on or mid-off trotting back to retrieve it from the boundary, I would sometimes find myself whispering 'good hall'.

Like lots of little boys who love hitting or kicking a ball, Ed was insatiable. When I had had more than enough of rolling it along the carpet to him in the winter months or bowling at him in the summer, when I needed to mark some essays or to push off to the pub, he would always ask for six more.

Last six, Dad.
And two more for luck.
No, can't finish on that, got to do better than that, one more.
Smack.
That'll do. Thanks, Dad.

Then, after a plateful of toast and jam and a Michael Jordan basketball video, he would move smartly in on his mother or his sister and I would soon hear bat on ball again.

Last six, Mum. Last six, Becky.
Come on, put a bit more into it.
Smack.

And it wasn't just at home that he practised. Each school holiday we travelled west (for a spell with his 'Welsh grandfather') but on the way we always turned off the M4, just before the Severn Bridge, and stayed with my wife's parents in Gloucestershire, where Ed would get more advice and more bowling, this time from his 'Yorkshire grandfather'. There they'd be in the garden, Eric then in his mid-seventies and Ed aged four or five, a grandfather and his grandson playing cricket, and I would be looking out of the patio doors to see my father-in-law assessing and suggesting and very occasionally (with his back to Ed) smiling his canny smile to himself.

This was also a weird and spooky re-run for me. It was sporting *déjà vu*, paramnesia, because thirty years earlier it had been much the same, only back then I was the young boy who Eric was trying to help. On summer evenings in the mid-1950s, after listening to Elvis or Buddy Holly or Eddie Cochrane, I used to go for grass nets with Eric. My older brother David, as cricket mad as I was, would come along too, and Eric (always padded up to bat first, box in, gloves on) would be there waiting with a half crown coin placed on top of the middle stump and, and while we bowled him into form for his weekend of Saturday and Sunday matches he would keep up the stream of instruction.

Eric's advice – to me in the 1950s or to Ed in the 1980s – was the best that any young cricketer of any generation could wish to hear, and you have to hear it in a Yorkshire accent:

-Come on, pitch it up, lad, you'll never get anyone out with that. Let it swing, better too full than too short. Don't lose your temper, Jonathan, you'll bowl worse. I told you you'd bowl worse, lad. Now calm down. That's more like it, had me in a bit of trouble there.

-*Howzat!*

-No, that's never LBW, not in Pudsey anyway. Len Hutton would never give that out, never. Don't try something new every ball. Wear me down. Be canny. Be patient. That's it, that's the spot. That's a length, that is. Why not just bowl a length? What's wrong with bowling a length? Don't have any fancy theories. There are too many fancy theories going round. Now that was a good ball. That was a good ball was that. That's what batsmen don't like. Why not give them what they don't like? You're not with the girls now.

And then, after he had filled his boots with all the batting practice he wanted, Eric would take his pads off and it was my brother David's turn to bat, and the stream of advice would continue as Eric started to bowl his medium pace seamers at him.

-Front foot closer. Smell the ball. Right forward or right back. Wrong ball for that shot, David. Bend that front knee. Yes, lad. That's it, I like the look of that. Hit it, that's rubbish, that is. That deserves all it gets.

While Eric would be plying his mean medium pacers at my determined brother I would be tiring badly and impatient to have a bat myself and, with nothing else working, I would now be trying to hit my brother on the body. Well, he had spent earlier years trying to hit me, hadn't he?

And then, with the light beginning to go and me getting more fretful and more disheartened, it would be time for Tom Graveney of Gloucestershire and England to bat. I put on my box and picked up my batting gloves. I could of course have been Colin Cowdrey or Peter May or any number of other top batsmen but there was no doubt about the player with whom I would identify. And as I walked into the nets I could hear Brian Johnston's rich tones as he described the match on the wireless.

-Yes, here is Tom Graveney coming down the pavilion steps now. And what a familiar sight he is, rosy faced, the elegant, tall right hander from Gloucestershire. How marvellous it would be for this big crowd if we were to see him unfurl some of his favourite off-side strokes.

And even against the fastest of fast bowlers Tom Graveney never seemed hurried. It was even the case when Hall and Griffith and the other West Indian quicks were battering the English top order. When the English top four seemed caught in the headlights, Tom somehow always had time.

Time, ah, time: that's the thing.

In sport Having Time is class. On stage, too, great actors always Have Time. Come to think of it, great performers in all arenas Have Time. And equally important (for me as a watcher) is that they Give Pleasure. The aesthetic side of sport is vital. Without elegance, without timing, without touch, without grace (the work ethic lot won't like that old-fashioned word, will they?), all games are much uglier and much the poorer.

And back in 1956 I was Tom Graveney, and I had my box on. It was not one of these modern plastic ones you slip into your jockstrap, it was one of those old-fashioned jobs, one of the padded boxes with white straps attached. It was a hell of a fiddle pulling the straps between your legs and under and round the back, especially if you were in the middle of a batting collapse and it's a bad wicket and you're next in and there's a big unshaven fast bowler running down the slope and the last man out is still running his bruised hand under the cold water tap and your own as yet unbruised fingers are already shaking and slightly sweaty.

T W Graveney, or Tom to you and me, played his first test for England against South Africa at Manchester in 1951. Manchester was the third test of that series. Strangely enough, Ed's first test was against South Africa in 2003, in the third test of the series, 52 years later.

Another thing. Tom always had the peak of his cap slightly raised, set just so, set at a slightly jaunty angle, and he always rolled his sleeves carefully up to just *below* the elbow, never right on the elbow and never ever above. Sleeves rolled right up above the elbow would have given him the blacksmith look and Tom wouldn't be seen dead as a blacksmith. Nor would I. I would never have dreamed of going out to bat or to field until I had my sleeves rolled up to exactly that point, Tom's point, *ie* just below the elbow. Yes, it was difficult to keep them rolled up and in place exactly there, because long sleeves tend to have a mind of their own and to work themselves loose, but that was the price of fame: attention to heroic detail.

I called out to my big brother – in a very genial way because Tom Graveney was always very genial – and asked him to give me guard:

-Middle and leg, please.

I was wasting my breath. Brother David did not even bother to turn round as he walked back to his mark. He called out,

-Doesn't make much difference where you stand.

-Yes, it does.

-No, it doesn't. Same result.

6

Agassi, father and son

Brothers aren't the real problem, though, not even my big brother. Fathers are. Well, not always, but far too often. As a teacher, whether I was the coach on the touchline or the umpire or the referee on the field of play, there was little doubt about the trickiest issue.

Boys could, of course, behave badly. They always have done and they always will do. They could let the team and themselves down by unfair or dirty play, poor body language, glaring at the umpire, graceless 'acceptance' of a decision, open dissent, shouting too much, spitting, throwing their bat and gloves and box before they got back to the pavilion, or saying 'would you fucking believe it' so loudly you could hear it, without the help of a following breeze, from fully sixty yards away. But all that was part of the job, and I found any or all of that easier to deal with than a particular kind of parental 'support'.

When a schoolboy had 'lost it' in the heat of battle I tried to make my point to him outside the changing rooms after the game. I would take him to one side for a quiet chat, the kind of quiet chat that involves only one speaker and one listener until things have become clear, and if that did not work and things remained unclear you could always drop him for the next match, or, if he still wasn't quite picking up the way the wind was blowing, you allowed him to go off and join the tennis club.

With some fathers, however, it was a different ball game. To be fair, most fathers get it right. They're there for the best reasons and with the best of intentions. Whatever the disappointments and the injustices out on the pitch, whatever the pain or the vicarious glory, most fathers turn up in a philosophical spirit to watch their children. They feel the thrill of seeing them play well, or, just as important, seeing them do their best, and they understand that their sons must accept all the ups and downs that go with the game. And the love between a father and son, often forged on the rocky road of sport, can run very deep.

But how does a teacher tell off a pushy parent who is so driven, so out of control, so doing his nut that it's gone way beyond prescription pills and may require sectioning? Faced with that kind of adult misbehaviour how does the teacher/coach make his approach? How does he shape his corrective sentences? Well, I never cracked that one. Much as you may fancy it you couldn't really go for the Alex Ferguson hairdryer, that's the dressing room full-on-toe-to-toe rant, the eye-rolling rollicking that blows the hairs right off the victim's head, nor could you drop Dad for next week's fixture, and, although I am out of touch with the latest Health and Safety requirements, as far as I am aware no touchline bans operate in school sport.

No, try as I might, I could never find the right way of explaining to that father just how off-putting and counter-productive his conduct was. And not only for his son, but also for his son's team and, while we're at it, for the referee and the opposition and the other parents, not to mention those living in the immediate neighbourhood, if he spent the afternoon bawling, lips frothing, like a man in the early stages of a seizure, not that I've ever seen a man in the early stages of a seizure, more like a man in the later stages of rabies then, not that I've seen that either but you can see his face, can't you, the saliva bubbles, the muscles at the corners of his mouth twitching, the difficulty with swallowing?

Most mothers were fine. Most mothers were absolutely great. They struck one as grown up. It was as if they understood that 'sport' and 'my son' and 'life and death' and 'tragedy and comedy' were concepts that came in different categories. There was, come to think of it, the occasional barking woman I can recall but no more than two or three in forty years.

Most women revealed – or settled for – an amused, semi-detached, supportive manner. Some looked slightly out of place, even a touch apologetic, as if they'd landed on an alien planet and were having some difficulty with the language. After a spot of patronising male explanation they might clap a successful moment – a try or a goal or a great tackle or a well struck boundary – but their body language tended to say: Yes, I know I'm being a bit silly being here at all but then it is all a bit silly, isn't it, but it means so much to them, and boys will be boys, and I'm a loyal mum and I'm also here to help keep things in proportion, but as long as my own lovely little boy is not too upset afterwards or, above all, not badly hurt I don't mind.

And a few of these same women would be deeply embarrassed at how their husbands were behaving, and would look away. As well they might.

Wouldn't you return to the car or turn your back and disown a man-boy who spent the whole afternoon walking round the boundary kicking the grass or pacing up and down the touchline shouting 'Ref! He's off side!' or 'This lot always cheat' or 'Never get a good ref here, do you?' or my least favourite, 'Oh, thank *you*, ref!', the father rolling his protruding eyes at the *cognoscenti* on the touchline and nodding to himself and clapping very slowly and sarcastically to make it crystal clear to all who had eyes to see, which would be nice if it included the ref, that after missing endless offsides/high tackles/late tackles/hands in the ruck and all of these by the opposition, that this particular referee (who was out of condition and couldn't even keep up with the game) had finally spotted an infringement and given a penalty, albeit far too late to affect the result.

Not that the father is finished yet. No, there's much more in the tank. At the end of the game he waits impatiently for his son to troop despondently off, and falls into step with him, and you hear him saying: 'Why did you play that shot/drop that catch/do that kick/make that pass/miss that tackle/how many times have I told you?'

It's as much as you can do not to run over and grab him by the shoulder and spin him round and say 'Look, what chance has he got if you go on being so one-eyed? Because I'll tell you. Sod all chance! Because he'll never be any good as a player if you bully him and dominate him and don't let him grow up' but even as you're thinking of doing this and saying this you pause mid-stride because you can feel a tap on your own shoulder and you can hear the whisper: 'Remember Mr Agassi?'

Mr Agassi?

Yes, I do.

Gulp.

And it's not a pretty story.

Andre Agassi's boyhood and adolescence and early manhood were all dominated by his father, Mike Agassi. As soon as Andre could walk his father put a tennis racket in his hand and had a machine fire hundreds and then thousands of tennis balls at him and in no time at all the lad was taking the ball early, counter-punching like a boxer, and on the way to being the best service returner the game has ever seen.

Mike Agassi terrified his whole family but he made Andre his special whipping boy. Worse, there were pills given, including amphetamines. He tried to turn his son on to speed. Later, in trying to cope, Andre tried crystal meth. His father never let up and put him through a prison camp regime until, and here's the difficult bit, Andre became a champion.

To put it delicately, Mr Agassi was an autocratic, bullying fanatic who forced his son through an abnormal childhood. But, at the risk of repeating the difficult bit, we do have to accept that he created a champion. In 1992, when Andre won Wimbledon, he rang his father and asked him what he thought.

No reply.

'Pops?'

'You had no business losing that fourth set.'

Andre Agassi won many grand slams, but he came to hate tennis. He was a winner who felt empty and dissatisfied. Was his father, as well as a bully, a soul-killer?

And, turning to a different sport, what did another father say of his even more famous son?

'Tiger will do more than any other man in history to change the course of humanity. He'll have the power to impact nations. Not people. Nations.'

We sporting fathers might recoil from Mike Agassi's conduct but it remains a troubling, if extreme, example. We might wince at Earl Woods' grandiose vision, but are many of us – including the one on a flight to India – just a bit better at masking our drives, more devious in our ambition to be the parents of winners, more civilised in our style, and more English in the manner of our obsession?

In the future, with the huge money now flowing into sport, will there be more and more children who have their minds and their bodies shamelessly damaged by the way they have been trained?

It's a hard one to call.

But we fathers are the problem, all right.

7

A good glare

I don't know how he found out, these things tend to get round, but Chris Cowdrey rang me the afternoon before Ed and I flew off to India. I have known Chris since he was a boy at Tonbridge School, that's forty years, and I can recognize his voice in a split second. Mind you, it's not difficult as he greets me with 'Author' and I sometimes reply 'Son Of'.

In the mid-1970s, when I was in my early thirties, I was running a small 'house' for twelve senior students, a kind of last chance saloon for twelve spirited individuals. That phrase, senior students, was an umbrella term we used for those boys who have their moments, those who have their ups and downs, those who are not mainstream, those who push the envelope, those who do not always fit hand in glove with a school's demands.

Some teachers call such pupils 'a handful' or settle for 'difficult'. Some prefer 'naughty' or 'not easy'. Some find them 'fun' or 'interesting' or 'lively'. The current word, usually delivered with an ironic edge, is 'challenging'. Whichever way you choose to describe them – and the whole point is that these individuals defy easy categories – they can stretch you to the limit: I lasted only seven years in that particular role because after seven years I found I was the one who was in need of a counsellor.

Not that there was such a person back then.

There were, however, enduring rewards. With quite a few of them, including Chris 'fun/lively' Cowdrey, I became friends. And of course I watched him play cricket on hundreds of occasions, at school and for Kent and for England. Over the years we phoned each other regularly and talked things through and found a lot to laugh at. And in 1985 we decided to team up and write a book together, a collaboration called *Good Enough?*

His father, Colin Cowdrey, was a player touched by genius, but because I had been a supporter of Tom Graveney since I was in short trousers I never really followed Colin in quite that way. With Chris it was different. With Chris Cowdrey it was personal: I had known him through his ups and downs and I cared, and when it comes to literature or to sport I have to care. However good they may be as writers or as players if I don't care I can't be bothered to turn the pages of their lives, can't be bothered to watch the ebb and flow of their game.

Anyway, whether he was on song or out of form, I followed Chris as I have followed very few others.

-Author!

-Son Of!

-Just heard the news.

-Ah, right.

-Bad luck.

-Ah well.

-We're thinking of you, Jonathan.

-Thanks.

-And I just want to say one thing to you, if that's all right?

-Fire ahead.

-Are you sure?

-Say whatever you like, Chris.

There was a pause.

-Not easy this. It's that I don't want you being nice about it, about what you're going through. I don't want you being passive and decent.

-OK.

-The thing is, I want you to glare at the batsman.

-I never was much of a glarer, Chris.

-Exactly. And that's my point. It's time for you to start.

-To start glaring?

-Yes. You've been hit unfairly. I want you to go down the

wicket and glare at him. He's swotted you and he shouldn't get away with it. I don't want you shrugging your shoulders and walking slowly back to your mark, all right?

-All right, I'll try that.

-Give him the glare.

-OK.

-Boycott did.

-Did he?

-Yes, when he got it Boycott glared.

-Right, OK. Hang on, had an idea, give me a second. I'll just pop upstairs. Right, going up the stairs. OK, I'm in the bathroom. And I'm now standing in front of the bathroom mirror.

-Good. So try it. Are you glaring?

-Yes I'm glaring.

-How are you coming over?

-Actually, it's not that bad.

-Really?

-I'll try again.

-Glare, Jonathan!

I tried another glare in the mirror.

-That one's better. In fact, I have to admit, that is quite a good glare. Can I go back downstairs now and make a coffee?

-You didn't mind me saying all that, did you?

-Of course I didn't.

-Bit of a cheek probably.

-No, you're right. It's a good thought, skip, good approach, top team talk.

-And you're off to India, I hear? With Ed?

-I am. Tomorrow.

-You'll love it.

-I'm sure I will.

-Remember me sending you all those tapes?

-As if it was yesterday.

-Fun, wasn't it?

Chris played in all five tests on England's 1984-85 tour of India and I do remember those unguarded and confidential tapes of his dropping through our letter box, tapes full of fun, full of liveliness, tapes from Madras and Delhi and Calcutta and Bombay and Kanpur. They formed part of a chapter in *Good Enough?*

And how can I forget those great moments:

Kapil Dev bowled Cowdrey 41
Azharuddin bowled Cowdrey 48

1984. Don't tell me, that's twenty years or more ago, and on those winter mornings, with patches of black ice on the drive, Ed and I sat huddled in our dressing gowns and listened to the Indian tapes together before going off to our different schools.

With Chris's voice in my ears it was as if I was on the inside track and very close to the action. I felt as if I was out there in India following the tour, surrounded by tens of thousands of fans in the colourful stands, with my eyes on Chris, my heart in my mouth, willing him to do well, as I watched the test matches unfold.

Ed, I sensed, was not in the stands but already out there in the middle, in the cauldron, asking the umpire for guard, 'Two please', looking round at the close catchers, then taking it ball by ball, and hoping the bad one would come along. He must have been seven.

8

Had he his hurts before?

When I was seven, way back in 1949, my father was the Headmaster of a state primary school on the northern outskirts of Bristol, and we lived in a very small house attached to the school. The house went with the job.

The School House, Patchway, it was called.

As a practice area for cricket my brother David and I may not have had grass nets but when my father rang the bell for the end of the school day we did have the playground all to ourselves. Then, as their voices died away, there would no more hopscotch or skipping, and we could get down to the serious stuff and play some cricket. And we played cricket, just the two of us, for hours on end in that yard. (We rarely went to the seaside for a holiday, and then it was only for a short stay in Porthcawl or Porlock, and we never went abroad.)

Each summer holiday morning, if it was dry, Dad was in his corduroys in the vegetable patch, corduroys worn shiny at the knees, and Mum in her apron was over the stove baking her pastries, blackcurrant tarts and damson tarts, and we were out in the yard chalking three wickets on the corrugated iron of the coal-house. As Dad was the Headmaster, whatever the other shortages of the early 1950s, at least there was plenty of chalk. My brother David, who was and who is very precise, emphatically re-marked the three stumps before each session of the day's play, particularly if I was batting.

We played with an orangey red ball. I can feel it in my fingers now. The ball was made of composition rubber, so it got smaller and smaller as the summer wore on and as the tarmac wore it away. There was no seam to pick, no need for ball tampering, no call for bottle tops or sharp nails, no need for sweat or sugar or lip salve, no skullduggery, no call for

Daryl Hair to check anything, no need for accusations of racism, no need at all to toss it to the umpire between the overs for closer inspection.

Sometimes chunks or bits or thin strips of it were knocked off, but usually the change in the ball's condition, its transformation, was less dramatic than that. It was like time passing. Slowly and imperceptibly, as August gave way to September, it was rubbed away and there was less and less to bowl with, less and less to get your fingers round: a bit like life, really.

Of course, the more disfigured the ball became the more unpredictably it behaved off the rutted tarmac, sheering left or sheering right or leaping up off a length, so that any bog standard delivery could prove a Frank Tyson bouncer or an off break as prodigious as Jim Laker's or a leg break as large and ludicrous as Shane Warne's famous first ball to Mike Gatting in 1993.

We did not have any pads to protect our legs. I did not put on a pair of pads until I was eleven. As for boxes, as for abdominal protectors, they were way in the future.

In the history of professional sport there is considerable evidence of the shaping influence of back yard sibling rivalry, of the conflict there has often been between competitive brothers. Take Jack and Bobby Charlton. It is sometimes called the younger brother syndrome, and for telling examples you have to look no further than the daily adolescent clashes and private duels between Ian and Greg Chappell, backyard confrontations that hardened and tested and forged those future world champions.

Am I saying, then, that the pressure of professional sport is a bit of a doddle after the bruising early years of fighting your brother in front of the coal-house?

I don't know, and the Smith brothers were certainly no future Chappells, but as I remember it – and though my memory may be dodgy in some areas it is top notch on pain recall – my brother David's main aim was to hit me. He'll deny it of course. He mounted a daily and focused bodyline attack on his irritating younger brother who was standing in front of the chalked stumps, the stumps he himself had chalked. If I cared to get out of the way and let the orangey red composition ball hit the stumps (with that tell-tale white chalk mark on the ball to prove the dismissal) that was fine by him because he would then be batting and batting for a very long time. But it was equally fine by him, and in some moods I suspected it was even finer, if I stayed in front of the chalked stumps and got hit on my bony shins.

We had no umpire, of course, no fatherly figure to see fair play. My father showed absolutely no interest in our sporting encounters. He was no Mike Agassi, my Dad. Years later he told me that he had once been 'hit by a cricket ball very hard, plumb in the privates' when he was a boy in the Rhondda Valley and once was quite enough thank you. From then on he was into snooker and billiards. Anyway, because there was no umpire in our school playground there was no LBW, but the lack of an umpire did not stop me showing my mother all the bruises on my shins (and also, I'm ashamed to say, the bruises on the back of my lacerated legs).

Old Siward has something to say about sons and courage in *Macbeth*. When, in Act 5, Scene 8, Old Siward is told that his son is lying dead on the field of battle all Old Siward wants to know is where exactly were his son's injuries: were his son's fatal injuries on his chest (*ie* on his front) or were they on his back? And hearing that his son's death wounds are all on his front Old Siward says well that's fine then, 'God's soldier be he', because apparently everything is just fine with Old Siward as long as Young Siward wasn't scarpering when he copped it:

SIWARD: Had he his hurts before?
ROSS: Ay, on the front.
SIWARD: Why then, God's soldier be he.

Looking at the bruises on the front and on the back of my legs, Mum asked David why he could not be kinder to me, sometimes (she said) our unkindness to each other made her wish she'd had not two sons but two daughters, and then she reminded David that his brother, the little coward, was three and a half years younger than he was but she also took me on one side and whispered that I didn't have to play cricket, did I, that if I didn't like being injured I could always help Dad dig the vegetable patch or I could be really nice and help her in the house or if neither of these options appealed I could always have a quiet time on my own and go up and lie on my bed and read *Children of the New Forest*, which my Aunty Eva who lived in Coventry had just given me.

I picked up the bat and David picked up the ball and we trooped back out to resume play in the school yard.

And when David had blasted me out, and it did not take him long, he went in to bat himself and dropped anchor. If I occasionally hit him on his bare legs he just leant on his bat and glared back at me. He never looked to see if there was a bruise or mentioned it or screamed or ran inside to tell Mum. Like Young Siward, his hurts were always on his front.

Perhaps he even liked being hit. It's possible. He could be a bit of a Brian Close. But like it or not, he had that look in his eye that said he was in for the duration and for all I know we'd still be there in that yard in Patchway Church of England Primary School now, me bowling and David batting, if August had not turned into September and in September we had to pack up cricket and go back to school, so at least I could escape this particular examination, except that September and a new school year meant the rugby season and more calls on my courage.

9

BA Flight 143

We identify with
We believe in
We follow
We love
We depend on
We live and die for

How deeply entwined the language of religion and
discipleship is with the language of psychology and sport. And
how one appropriates and calls on the other. In professional
football matches when someone scores a special goal large
numbers of the fans start to sway together in adulation and to
hail their idol with we-bow-down-before-him gestures, and as
the goal scoring messiah runs towards the corner flag and
slides down on his knees before the adoring multitude they
respond by glorifying his name with a chant.

My mind side-steps and, quite unbidden, Bob Dylan is
starting to sing *I Believe in You*. The version I am hearing is not
the *Slow Train Coming* recording but the 1979 *Saturday Night
Live* performance. The simple line in the song may appear the
same on the page but, as he sings it, Bob Dylan infinitely
varies the emphases and so the meaning. He might sing:

I believe in you.
or
I be-*lieve* in you.
or
I believe in *you*.
or
And I believe in you.
or
And I believe in you.

And though I could not see right down there, I believed we were now passing over Belgium.

During the first part of our night flight, with Ed asleep beside me, I found myself slipping back again to that suburban school yard in north Bristol and to the developing nature of my dependency. It was a little boy dependency that became adolescent dependency before I came to realize that I was in for the long haul. The names of the sportsmen and the writers I have identified with and followed may have changed and the list has certainly got longer as I extended my allegiance into other fields, but I have never grown out of the mindset, of the heart-stopping thrill and anxiety of wanting to see my heroes win their battles and win the day.

I was also thinking more specifically how the back yard games I played with my brother David had led by a winding route to this particular journey, and even more so how curious it was that a father and a son, over fifty years later – brought together by fate, by family, by cricket – should be sitting side by side on Flight 143 to Delhi, while in just a few weeks time my brother would be on the same flight path.

In the winter months David and his friends, most of them dating back to schooldays, like to follow England's overseas cricket tours: they go to the West Indies or to South Africa or, in this instance, to India. The very antithesis of The Barmy Army they are a quiet Welsh group, The Welsh Corner, and they watch every ball. They often find they are booked in to the same hotel as the players, so I pick up bits of gossip, which players couldn't have been nicer to say hullo to and which players wouldn't give you the time of day.

Going on a journey of any length always makes me think. Perhaps it goes with the territory. Walking is obviously the best for reflection and for the rhythms of creativity, but if I am travelling on a boat or a train or a plane (less so a car) I cannot help seeing it as a metaphor. For example, if only my own life had followed the clear and confident path that this aeroplane is taking. You book in and you board the plane and you trust in the pilot (we are in his hands, as I will soon be in the hands of the anaesthetist and the surgeon) and you set off and you follow the pre-ordained path and you arrive. There might be a little turbulence. You might have to fasten your seat belt for a few bumpy rides, but it's usually nothing more than that, and the journey has a purpose and it has a narrative with a clear end in view. You don't get lost. And as for the aeroplane falling out of the sky, I never think about it.

I wish I could say the same of my own life journey. I have only too vividly feared problems and all too often 'seen' many crashes on the road ahead of me, crashes that usually never happened. Or is that what they now call 'defensive pessimism'? I heard them talking about that on Radio Four the other day and I thought yes, that's what I've got, defensive pessimism, and it cheered me up no end.

At the moment, though, I am following our progress, the easterly movement of BA Flight 143 to Delhi, following it on the little screen fixed on the back of the seat in front of me. My geography is not too hot so I am learning something every inch of the way. It is faintly ridiculous that I have such a detailed grasp of the most minor cricket statistics, such as the batting averages of my school team in 1959, and that I also know the quarto and folio variant readings of some key passages in Shakespeare (when any normal fool would settle for one or the other) and yet despite the television news I know next to nothing about well, let's say, China, and I've barely started to get to grips with the whole region they call the Balkans, and I'm more or less lost on much of Africa and South America. I hope it's not just that they don't play much cricket in those places.

It is a worry to me that at the very moment when the world finally blows up I could well be checking the county cricket scores on Ceefax. The country is on red alert and they have given the three minute warning but I missed it as I was tapping in the numbers on my television handset and waiting for the right panel to flicker up. As I tap away my heart is beginning to jump ahead. Will the name I am looking for, will E Smith, often the first name in the batting order, be in white (which means he is not out, still in, still batting, and if he is still batting has he got 3 or 53, 100 would be very nice indeed of course but I'll settle for 40, 40 is always acceptable, 40 is not a bad day at the office, shall we settle for 40?) or has his name turned to blue (meaning he is out, and if he is out then being run out for 0 would be the worst case scenario)?

My heart is going.

When I see his name will it be a moment of acclaim or commiseration, triumph or grief?

Ah, here it comes:

BOOM.

Instead of looking at the computerized progress of our flight I could of course be re-reading the poems and anticipating his questions on them, or I could be watching a film. The woman in front of me, for example, is watching *The Constant Gardener*. I saw it just off Leicester Square. Indeed if I lean slightly to the right I can see Ralph Fiennes and Rachel Weiss making love.

When I was showing a video in my teaching days (with cricket practice looming) and there was a sex scene in the film, and since you ask me yes one such scene does spring to mind, the scene in the Australian creek when the young Jenny Agutter is being secretly watched by an aboriginal teenage boy as she takes her clothes off and swims, *Walkabout* the film was called, 1971, directed by Nicholas Roeg, screenplay by Edward Bond, and the aboriginal was played by David Gulpilil, my class would ask if I would mind very much rewinding the tape a bit, oh go on, sir, but I always told them to grow up. One boy would then say that he was growing up but it was proving a very slow and so far disappointing business and another boy would say that his parents had told him nothing at all and on research grounds alone a rewind would be really helpful, so I reminded them that they should be concentrating on their course work essay which is due in next Tuesday that's next Tuesday not next Wednesday and let me remind you all that the title of the essay is 'The plight of the aboriginal in a post-colonial world'.

-Sir!

-Aww, come on, sir!

In fact I could have rewound the tape and showed them Jenny Agutter all over again, and I might indeed rewind the tape and watch it all over again but that would only be after they had all gone home and I had locked my classroom door and had pulled down the blind and was safe.

Meanwhile the real aeroplane we are sitting in flies on at 600 or thereabouts miles per hour through the night skies. And meanwhile my tiny unromantic aeroplane cursor is moving oh-so-slowly across the little screen. Before too long it will be Turkey down there, I've seen a few Turkish films, they don't come much better than *Yol* and then, well God knows what's next, is it Iraq and Iran, or is it Iran and Iraq, I've forgotten in which order they come, no I haven't forgotten, the thing is I never knew.

When I'm asked a question about something I ought to know about I often smile and say isn't it terrible I used to know the answer but I'm sorry to say I have forgotten it (age, you know, age), which is playing on the sympathy vote that once upon a time I was pretty formidable on that sort of thing but now I am going a bit at the edges, having a bit of a senior's moment, whereas the plain truth is that I never had a mortal clue what the answer was in the first place.

Just before he fell asleep Ed asked,

-These poems you've brought?

-What about them?

-They're not the sort no-one can understand, are they?

-You'll have to wait and see, won't you?

And talking of poems and novels, and talking of literary heroes, when we get to Delhi we are going out to dinner with Vikram Seth. Vikram has asked us over to his place for the evening. It is a while since I've seen him, and I cannot think of a better way to begin this Rajasthan jaunt.

10

-Right, I said, before we land, here's the first one I've
 brought.
-Who's going to read it?
-You are.

Don't ask me...

Don't ask me;
I have no recipe
for a poem. You
know the language,

know where prose ends
and poetry begins.
There should be no
introit into a poem.

The listener should come
to and realise
verse has been going on
for some time. Let

there be no coughing,
no sighing. Poetry
is a spell woven
by consonants and vowels

in the absence of logic.
Ask no rhyme
of a poem, only
that it keep faith

with life's rhythm.
Language will trick
you if it can.
Syntax is words'

way of shackling
the spirit. Poetry is that
which arrives at the intellect
by way of the heart.

R S Thomas (1913-2000)

Deep down I knew I would not get away with it, and I didn't, because this poem was never going through on the nod. Being an English teacher I was anticipating the old classroom chestnut, 'But is this poetry? Isn't it chopped up prose?' a question often edged with animus, and I had braced myself for the argument about rhyme and form and free verse that would ensue. But that wasn't Ed's line at all.

Instead, as we lowered and lurched down on Delhi airport, he said it was good that I had started with a Welsh poet but just how Welsh was R S Thomas. Was he Anglo-Welsh like Edward Thomas and Wilfred Owen? Or, was he a bit over-the-top-Welsh-Welsh-but-not-actually-Welsh-speaking-Welsh like Swansea's own Dylan Thomas, drunk on words down in his boathouse in Laugharne?

Well, R S Thomas was born in Cardiff to an English speaking family but his parents moved up to North Wales and he went to university at Bangor. Aged thirty, while speaking English with a cut-glass Oxford accent, he taught himself Welsh. Indeed he taught himself his second language so thoroughly that he wrote *Neb*, his autobiography, in the third person in Welsh, which then had to be translated back into English.

-So, Ed says, a bit of a nutter as well?

-Not sure, not sure. But odd, definitely odd.

Seamus Heaney somewhere calls R S Thomas a Clint Eastwood of the spirit, and I like that. Think *Unforgiven*. Think of bleak hills and chapels and uncommunicative shepherds. Imagine an outlandish man lost to creature comforts, a stern preacher with a mad glint in his eye, a Welsh nationalist who sent his only son to Bradfield, a very English public school. Think, if you will, of a taciturn priest striding past you, a prophet with his long white hair blowing in the wind, an ascetic who insisted on living in a bitterly cold house in a remote parish and then, in case his wife was starting to feel too comfortable, had the central heating torn out and the Hoover dumped because it was too noisy.

-Great. Even grumpier than Larkin, then?

-Close call. But only a top class player can write: 'Poetry is that/which arrives at the intellect/by way of the heart.' And Denis Healey likens Thomas's late poetry to Beethoven's last quartets. So he's on the team sheet.

11

A one-footed boy

When I was a boy in Wales – this was before J P R Williams and Gareth Edwards and Barry John and Gerald Davies, and well before I got seriously into poetry – I tried very hard to be good at rugby and cricket. Cricket and rugby were my games, if that does not sound proprietorial, and I spent thousands of hours determined to develop my all round performance and to prove to myself and to the many doubters amongst my schoolmates that I was a decent player.

How important was it for me to be thought a decent player? How about life and death?

I was a full back, *ie* I wore the Number 15 shirt. Not that we actually had numbers on the back of our schoolboy shirts in the 1950s, all that schoolboys in team tracksuits and all that trying to look professional stuff was still way in the future, but on the basis of my position alone I stood in the long and distinguished line of full backs that led to J P R Williams.

So what kind of player was I?

Well, I could kick well with my left foot, punt to touch well, torpedo (or screw kick) and place kick at goal from reasonable distances. I also worked very hard on my right foot because I did not want to favour my left and to be called one-footed. 'Smith's one-footed' would be a big put-down. What else? I caught the high ball easily, and I 'could pass off both hands'.

The trouble was I lacked pace, or, as one of my coaches liked to stress, I wasn't *quick*, and being quick was even better than being fast. In rugby, it wasn't about who won the hundred yards sprint, it was the speed of your reactions that mattered, your alertness, your sharpness of mind and foot.

What's more, I was not a strong tackler, and in the very exposed position of full back (as the game was then played) it showed. There was no hiding place. You were a lone tree in the desert. At full back you were the last line of defence and if you had a bad game, and having a bad game usually meant you had knocked the ball on under your own posts or had missed the crucial tackle, you stood out like a sore thumb.

For a season or two, I did tackle in a kind of kamikazi way, self destructively crashing head first into the advancing three quarters but quite often only succeeding in doing more damage to myself than to the opposition. There I was, flat on my back staring up at the referee and my team-mates or (in later days at Cambridge) in Addenbrooke's Hospital. It clearly hadn't worked because the whole idea had been to put the other person in hospital.

There is, of course, a kind of over-the-top mad courage in sport that only serves to mask fear. The lower order batsman, for example, the blacksmith type who rolls his sleeves up above the elbows and swaggers out to the crease from the pavilion and smashes the quick bowlers to all parts of the ground is often scared stiff underneath. As a bowler I could often smell this fear on the lower order slogger from twenty two yards away.

A soldier I knew (who went to my school and was later decorated in the Falklands for extreme bravery in the face of enemy fire) told me that when he leapt up out of his trench with his gun and stormed forward he had (i) lost his temper and (ii) lost all self control, but more than either of those (iii) he 'could not stand it any more'.

Whether I was brave or not, I could marshal the on-field tactics quite well, and return kicks with interest and generally keep things tight, but I could never slice through a defence, and desperately keen though I was I could never win or even change a game, though I did once (on a very windy and wet day) save a game by making a great mark to an up-and-under kick (called a Garryowen in those days), which was swirling around and coming down right in front of our posts, always a tricky part of the pitch because the ball can bounce off one of the posts, off the cross bar or the uprights, and go anywhere, sometimes leading to a soft try, but I caught it cleanly and dug my heel in and called 'Mark!' (and all done at the same time, as you then had to) just before I was buried by some hairy scrum-capped forward with his elbow in my throat and I got to my feet and made the clearance punt to touch on the 25 yard line and that can take a bit of doing from under the posts with a heavy ball on a wet and windy day (*and* the balls were heavier then, much heavier) and at the final whistle I was even congratulated by our coach who had played fly half for Wales and was not all that keen on congratulating anyone least of all a one-footed full back who couldn't really play.

(Actually, just writing that last long sentence about my JPR moment in 1959 – come to think of it JPR would have been aged nine at the time – makes me feel quite proud.)

On the pitch I partly made up for my deficiencies by adroit positioning and by anticipating the next move. And here my literary critical mind may well have helped because I could often read the game. I had a feel for it, for the narrative. Sometimes I could see how it was unfolding a split second before others did and on an instinct I could pop up in attack or defence at the right time and in the right place and (to the casual observer) even seem to be the instigator of a move.

But all that anticipating/reading the game stuff only takes you so far, and at the higher reaches of sport only so far isn't very far. The simple truth is that from the age of twelve to twenty two, while being very critical of everyone else, I did not realize that basically I was no good. I did make my school Ist XV for one season but I was no good at any level that satisfied me, no good that is at any level that I was content to play at. So, at twenty three, as teaching took over my life, I gave up playing rugby and started to coach it.

My journey in cricket, which in a sense is still going on, has been longer and more difficult, though I can now see that there are some common threads. From the age of eight I wanted to be a batsman. Well, as you know, I was Tom Graveney, wasn't I?

When I was batting I could sometimes time the ball quite sweetly on the off side. I could 'put away' a long half volley with the best of them, but then so can most people who can play at all, and I had little to offer off the back foot. And on the slow pitches of mid Wales that was fatal. I tended to lunge forward and get locked into a bad position, which meant I played across my pads and got given out LBW, but back in the pavilion the LBW decision was always the easiest part to explain. The umpires couldn't umpire, could they? They were crap, all of them were, but particularly this one.

Given all of the above, it is not surprising that I found it difficult to deal with the short ball or the rising ball. And I found it even more difficult after I had my front teeth knocked out on the afternoon before I took one of my A level papers in English literature. Paper Three I think it was. Paper One was Shakespeare, two plays studied in great detail. Paper Two was Chaucer and Milton. Paper Three was a syllabus of the Metaphysical Poets, ed. Helen Gardner, Dryden's *Absalom and Achitophel*, Johnson's *Vanity of Human Wishes* and Pope's *The Rape of The Lock*.

My God, I've just again looked at that list, Dryden, Dr Johnson and Pope: I bet they don't teach any of that lot now, not with all the coursework they need to hand in on Women War Poets on the Western Front. If you went into class now and said right, everyone, just to say that this term we're doing the Metaphysical Poets, that's Donne, Herbert, Vaughan, Marvell and a few others, and then we're doing Dryden and Pope and after that Dr Johnson, they'd be straight on their mobiles to their mums and changing their A levels at lunchtime.

Anyway, in cricket practice one afternoon I had played forward to a ball I should of course have played back to, as my coach explained while we were looking for my teeth in the dusty crease. There was a crack and a crunch and a burn and a split and my tongue felt a big gap and a thick top lip and I was sitting on my haunches spitting blood into my handkerchief and all over my Lillywhite pads.

-Why did you play forward to that, Smith?

-Don't know, sir.

-I've told you often enough, haven't I?

-Yes, sir.

-About lunging forward to short balls?

-Yes, sir, sorry.

-No point in you trying to be a batsman if you're never going to listen. Is there?

-No, sir.

The boy who bowled the ball, sharpish left arm over and the best player in our side, was very upset, which is more than the invigilator handing out the question papers the next morning was, a teacher who liked to think that he was a bit of a Welsh wit and a bit of a Welsh wag.

-Ah, and who do we have here? *Drac*-u-la? No, no, it's *Fran*-ken-stein, isn't it?

After this and a number of visits to the dentist, I was back playing cricket, and back at the batting crease. Sad to say, I never got right behind the ball again, because having your front teeth knocked out at seventeen was quite clear enough proof for me that I had shown some courage and had got right behind the ball and look where getting right behind the ball had landed me: in the dentist's chair, with my tongue exploring a very wide and very unpleasant gap.

But even with this injury, and even with the annual and mounting career evidence of my averages, I was twenty six before I realized that not only was I not Tom Graveney, I was not even a batsman of the most basic kind.

So how on earth can I have been in denial for so long?

There is something about sport, about playing sport, especially playing sport if you're a follower and a fan, that means you often cannot see the truth about your own game. You could call this sad or hilarious or worrying or disturbing, but you are often blind about yourself, and I have seen overwhelming evidence of this on village greens and on school fields and in parks and in the nets and in back gardens. They come out of the pavilion, these batsmen, beautifully kitted up, and they walk out to the middle and take careful guard and look knowingly around at the disposition of the fielders or they come on to bowl and very precisely mark out their run up like a pro but they are hermetically sealed inside their own self delusion, and if you are into doing the decent thing – as quite a lot of cricketers are – you must not by word or deed or sign disabuse them.

And when they are bowled neck and crop first ball or drop a dolly catch or bowl six full tosses or long hops in a row you have to say 'Bad luck'. You must not, above all, smirk. If on such occasions I feel that I have to say something to the deluded player, if I have to say something to his disbelieving and self-pitying face, my preferred line has always been: 'Don't worry, we all have days like this.'

Anyway, back to my late conversion to being a bowler. Between the ages of twenty-six and forty-five I spent my time bowling rather than batting. Better a conversion that comes late rather than never. I became what you might call a controlled away swing bowler, barely medium pace at best, and I developed a slower ball (or an even slower ball) and also one that cut back (or at least held its line, which means it goes straight on).

On special days, and every dog has his day, even a medium pace swing bowler has his moment in the sun. There were sessions or spells or a sequence of deliveries when I could make the ball 'talk' ie do exactly what I wanted it to do. Then I would take a handful of top order wickets, even surprising a star batsman who I sensed had written me off as innocuous only to find himself walking back to the pavilion shaking his head, with his body language saying, or even his mouth quite clearly saying to the incoming batsman:

'How on earth did I get out to shit like that?'

On those rare days I loved proving the people who had underrated me wrong. *Days Like This* is one of my favourite Van Morrison songs. And on days like this, when I made the ball talk, I felt a truly wonderful glow. For a brief moment I demonstrated that I had mastered a skill, or at least some aspects of the skill of bowling. All the hours of hard practice in the nets, bowling alone in the fading light at a white handkerchief pinned to the pitch, had paid off. I was getting better. Just as all the solitary hours in my bedroom or in the library with Dickens or Mrs Gaskell had made me a better reader, those long sessions on my own in the nets had worked. Look at the evidence in the score-book.

On days like that I felt that I wasn't completely out of my depth on the sporting stage. I felt, in the grudgingly generous Aussie phrase, that 'I could play a bit'. And one giddy Saturday morning in an all day game I bowled out the opposition before lunch and I was asked to lead the side off the field, and I did, and they clapped me into the pavilion, and I wouldn't have minded an idiot reporter from Sky Sports shoving a microphone in my face and interviewing me, but no luck there, so I told the guys they could take a photo of me as well if they liked, and they did. Wish I knew where it was.

12

Round and Round

After a long and wretched flight
That stretched from daylight into night,
Where babies wept and tempers shattered
And the plane lurched and whisky splattered
Over my plastic food, I came
To claim my bags from Baggage Claim.

Around, the carousel went round
The anxious travellers sought and found
Their bags, intact or gently battered,
But to my foolish eyes what mattered
Was a brave suitcase, red and small,
That circled round, not mine at all.

I knew that bag. It must be hers.
We hadn't met in seven years!
And as the metal plates squealed and clattered
My happy memories chimed and chattered.
An old man pulled it out of the Claim.
My bags appeared: I did the same.

Vikram Seth (1952-)

13

Horn pleas

I just missed National Service, and with it any outside chance of being an officer in the army, so being saluted as we walked into the Imperial Hotel, Delhi, by a big man in a white uniform with a large handlebar moustache was the first, but only the first, of many such salutes I received on the steps of Indian hotels. I have to say I never quite overcame my embarrassment at every one of them.

Ed laughed at my discomfiture, as he likes to do, and suggested it would be much better 'to sit back and enjoy'. A bit of deference, that's what you need, Dad. But being driven through those avenues of king palms and stepping out of taxis or cars I felt I had been mistaken for minor royalty. In return to the Indian salute I settled for something clumsy, a gesture somewhere between an honestly-no-no-you-really-shouldn't shake of the head and a low-key civilian wave.

Still, it was nowhere near as embarrassing as an incident at Philip Larkin's Memorial Service in 1986 when I was standing to one side on the steps of Westminster Abbey only to be mistaken by a gaggle of press photographers for Ted Hughes. The more I protested that I wasn't Ted Hughes the more the photographers were convinced that I was Ted Hughes, Ted Hughes being modest, Ted Hughes being a bit difficult at Philip Larkin's Memorial Service, so I ran down the steps as fast as I could and was off and away but they only ran after me, their cameras clicking.

On the journey into Delhi from the airport, everything over-reached anything my over-active imagination had ever imagined. It was to prove the same wherever I went in India. Even so, in those first few moments my eye – as my eye tends to do – kept focusing on silly things. The first small silly thing

was the sign stuck on the backs of the lorries, the lorries jammed right across the road ahead, and it was the same sign on the backs of the cars and the cycle rickshaws and the auto-rickshaws and the Eco Friendly Bus Companies.

Keep distance!
Horn please!
Blow horn!

And the one I liked best of all:

Horn pleas!

But did they keep distance?

No, no one kept distance, no room to keep distance, and did they blow horn, yes, everyone blew horn. People were hanging on to bumpers and to buses, and there were more passengers packed into and hanging out of and clinging on to one vehicle than seemed possible.

New Delhi and Old Delhi, two worlds.

Wide avenues and parks and planned vistas and Parliament buildings suddenly gave way to thousands of bicycles criss-crossing the narrow packed streets. Little bonfires, or were they small refuse dumps, burned on the pavements, and old men sat motionless and cross-legged. Then I could no longer look out at the streets because up there, right up there was the Red Fort, a fort bigger than any I had ever seen, more a city in itself than a fort, a palace as fortified as any your imagination could make up.

On many street corners, high above the shops, there were huge posters (thirty or more feet high) of the Indian cricket stars:

Rahul Dravid
Sachin Tendulkar
Virender Sehwag
Sourav Ganguly
Anil Kumble
and many others.

-They're pretty big out here, Ed said.

These towering portraits were advertising the current test series between India and Pakistan as well as the one coming up between India and England. Ed was lucky enough to play with Rahul Dravid, a modest and delightful man, when he was at Kent – I saw them bat together a number of times in 2000 – and Rahul sent Ed a text message in August 2003 when he was picked for England. Indian cricketers, as the posters make clear, have a prestige and a film star glamour in their own country unrivalled by cricketers or indeed sportsmen anywhere in the rest of the world. Indian cricketers are not just *followed*: they are gods.

When I was young I did not, I have to admit, take Indian cricket at all seriously. Indian cricket never came into my frame: a poor reflection on me and my upbringing perhaps, but that is how it was. When I played table cricket (a game requiring only the roll of a dice, a scorebook, a boring maths lesson, a pencil and a propensity to cheat) it was always Lindwall and Miller, the famed Australian fast bowlers, who were running in full tilt to bowl at Tom Graveney and Peter May, or Len Hutton and Colin Cowdrey.

If asked I could not have come up with any of the Indian bowlers who would be a serious challenge to the stars of my cricketing world. The Australians were, of course, deadly serious. The South Africans were serious. With Weekes, Worrell and Walcott the West Indians were becoming serious.

The New Zealanders were always serious, but that was only on the rugby field.

Whether or not the salutes on the porch steps were to be taken at face value I was more than ready for the Imperial Hotel, Delhi. Contemporary colonial (with a hint of ironic charm) was the house style and our large cool room was hung with prints of tiger shoots and an imperial past: on one wall there was 'Colonel Sir Arthur Ellis at close quarters with a tiger, April 1st 1876', while on another I saw 'The Prince of Wales shooting with Sir Jung Bahadoor'.

14

Watching Tom

-So, who do you follow?

It is a question I often find myself asking people, and the response I tend to get is:

-*Follow?*

-Yes.

-No one says that any more.

-Don't they?

-No, people say *support*. What people say now is: 'Who do you support?'

-Do they?

-Yes.

-But that misses the point.

-What point?

-Well, the discipleship, the religious dimension, the footsteps, the inadequacy, the pilgrimage, the follow-my-leader. It misses all that. 'Supporting' doesn't quite capture it. Following is much more interesting, and much more disturbing.

Being a follower is a bit like being in love, and try telling someone in love that they're getting it all terribly wrong. Following exerts a great, if not an appalling, pull. Following follows that falling-in-love arc, that falling-in-love curve. It usually starts young, starts tentatively, with shyness, with devotion and idealization, with wish-fulfilment from afar. By stages it develops from that wide-eyed infatuation, from seeing only the good things, to identification and compulsion.

Like falling in love it can happen, of course, at any age and on any day and often leads to full-on obsessive behaviour and excessive mood swings. And telling myself to pull myself together does not work either, any more than it works if someone else tells me to pull myself together. I have given myself the final big father-to-son-talking-to thousands of times.

****

I first saw Tom Graveney walk out to bat on a cloudy day (a typically Bristol day) in August 1952. I was ten and a half and in short trousers. Tom was then twenty five, which is four years younger than Ed is now. That is hard to believe. And a year later, in 1953, the year we regained the Ashes, Tom Graveney was a Wisden Cricketer of the Year. That is not so hard to believe.

With my packet of sandwiches and my big bottle of Tizer lemonade I caught the Gloucester to Bristol bus down the A38 – there was a bus stop right outside our house which meant that Mum did not have to worry about me so much – and I got off twenty five minutes later at Nevil Road. I walked along the narrow streets to the county ground and through the Grace gates and into a new world, a world of score cards and obsessive detail, a home for hero worship and (coming up soon) superstition.

I sat – as I still do at any ground – as close as I could get to the boundary (*ie* right under the old scoreboard and facing the orphanage) and in no time at all I was tucking into my cheese and tomato and Branston Pickle doorsteps. I liked doorstep sandwiches then and I like doorstep sandwiches now: at a cricket match I find I still eat most of my food an unhelpfully long time before lunch. For some reason I cannot just sit there and watch the cricket and glance down at the newspaper and forget all about the doorsteps. As for the lemonade, I used to drink it straight from the top of the bottle, but that is a habit of mine that my children have over the years managed to break.

So there I was in my Clark's sandals and my Aertex shirt sitting as close to the boundary as I could get and eating my sandwiches and swigging my Tizer and watching T W

Graveney stroke it to all parts of the ground, easing it through the covers or pulling off the front foot to leg, and all the while I was, as you know, imagining that T W Graveney was me and that I was Tom Graveney. I didn't know the word then, but I identified.

Was I happy?

Was I happy!

It was only when I went to the lavatory and returned to my seat to find that T W Graveney was out, caught behind and already back in the pavilion, that my happiness on that day came to a sudden end and I took another step on the follower's road and began my lifetime of superstition.

Because somebody in Bristol should have got hold of me and told me there and then the simple thing that I had done wrong. By going to the lavatory I had left my seat. I had moved. As a spectator at a cricket match you must never move when things are going well, and most particularly you must never move when your favourite player is batting.

You think I'm joking?

I'm serious.

Never, ever.

But if I need to go to the lavatory?

Too bad. Put up with it. I am deadly serious.

Don't move!

If you do, on your own head be it.

Wet yourself if you have to.

15

Coriolanus

I first met Vikram Seth in 1969. He must have been about sixteen; I was twenty seven. We used only surnames for our pupils in those days so I would have called him 'Seth', pronounced phonetically. I notice that many in English literary circles now use the Indian pronunciation 'Sate', another significant sign. Should I stick to 'Seth' or go with 'Sate'?

Anyway, in 1969 there was a new boy in my class, an Indian.

-Morning, Seth isn't it?

-Yes, sir.

-And you've come here from The Doon School?

-I have, yes.

If he had cared to correct me on the pronunciation of his name he did not. Perhaps he did not mind. Perhaps he was being polite. Perhaps he accepted the world as it was.

Vikram joined Tonbridge School in the sixth form – in the opening section of his book *Two Lives* he gives his account of those days – and I was teaching him, if that is the word, for his Oxbridge entrance examinations. It took me less than fifteen minutes to sense that the boy Seth would not be needing me or anyone else to help him achieve this end, but that realization only made the lessons with him all the more exciting. And when I was sitting at home later that week, reading the first essay he had handed in to me, I felt my hands tremble.

I had set him Aufidius's famous speech from Act IV, Scene, xi in *Coriolanus* (*'All places yield to him 'ere he sits down'*, you know the passage). It is quite a challenge even to paraphrase that speech in clear modern English, and a challenge I often like to set pupils who intend to read English at university. What is Aufidius saying here about his great enemy Coriolanus, and what might Shakespeare be suggesting in general about the nature of a tragic character, not only Coriolanus himself but all tragic characters? Does one serious weakness in our natures override and cancel out all our virtues? Are you to be written off as a cricketer if, say, you have a weakness against leg spin or get shaken up by a well-directed bouncer? Does that weakness mean that all your other strengths are as nothing?

Reading Vikram's response to Aufidius's speech from *Coriolanus* was not the first nor the last time that I felt that thrill, that tell-tale tremble in my hands. Reading wonderful writing from a pupil is one of the joys of the teacher's life, as well as one of the compensations for the thousands of hours of marking, and in more recent years for the drearily industrial hours of form filling and box ticking.

And, when you are reading something *that* good you slowly put the essay down, your hands fall to your side, and you stand up and you walk around your room and you pick the essay up again and you read it through once more just to be quite sure that you haven't allowed yourself to be carried away and overrated it (and you haven't) and you notice for the second time the sharp but light touch, the penetrating point, the elegance of the phrasing, the flick of the wrist, the quickness of mind, the range of shots, the sense of a hidden armoury, the timing and the feel of the sentences, the ease of the comparisons, the sense that really hard work has been done but that somehow it has all been made to look easy, the art that hides art, it could be Tom Graveney, it could be Tom making 267 against the West Indies, or it could be Barry John, the Welsh fly half of the 1970s, gliding so easily through a packed defence, and you whisper 'Wow! How about that!' to yourself and you look out of the window and you nod to yourself and say out loud to the empty room,

-Has this guy got it or what!

Then, because you are so excited, you ring up a colleague (or two) and you say listen to this and you read out bits from the essay and they say: 'Yes, blimey, I see what you mean, Jonathan, sounds like we might have a bit of a genius on our hands here. What's his name again?'

'Seth. He's Indian.'

Vikram Seth, the Indian, who would later write poetry and travel books and great novels:

The Humble Administrator's Garden
From Heaven Lake
The Golden Gate
All You Who Sleep Tonight
A Suitable Boy
Beastly Tales From Here and There
An Equal Music
Two Lives

Vikram has just returned from a long promotional tour of North America, in and out of every major city, doing interviews and readings all across the States, and is now spending some time with his parents and his family before setting off on the next leg, this time to South America.

The last time I saw him was at the launch of *Two Lives* in London. I am annoyed, though, because as soon as I sit down at the table I am hit by pole-axing uncontrollable tiredness. I give myself a pep talk but I can hardly sit up straight, and I find my mind has slowed almost to a halt. I am struggling badly. Quite simply, I have 'gone'. There is nothing I can do about it. I'll just eat.

Above all I do not want to be asked what my first impressions of India are because all I have to offer are the clichés you read a few pages back. Never mind, the table talk is about books and careers and influences and chance and injustice and how and when we started on our chosen paths. Vikram's father asks me when I first noticed that Ed could play cricket – a question I have often had to field – and then he asks me a father's question, how difficult is it to watch him, how do you feel as you sit there in the stands?

****

I don't know where to start, Mr Seth.

But I can't say that. And I can't say it's the pain.

'Are you a masochist or what?' That was how a friend put it to me when I was going on about what a nightmare Ed's recent run of low scores had been, and why, when he's batting in the gloom, why do the umpires always delay going off for bad light until he gets an edge and is caught, and then they offer the light the very next ball.

Why is the game so perverse?

Why is it that when you, as a batsman, already have a row of low scores against your name you then get the one jaffa, the very best ball bowled on that day? Worse than that, much worse than that, how is it that when some medium paced dibbly dobbly bowls a loopy long hop down the leg side, possibly the worst ball bowled that day, it brushes your gloves and goes through to the keeper? And why is it that when everyone else nicks the ball it goes harmlessly through the slips and runs safely away for a deeply undeserved four but the first time you nick it second slip leaps like a salmon and takes a quite breathtaking tumbling catch?

Come on, Shakespeare, explain that!

And what about when the umpire has given you out LBW but Hawkeye shows very clearly that the ball was going on to miss leg stump or going well over the top?

LOOK, my friend said. Look, he said, it's very easy, you can walk away from it all, turn your back on cricket, don't go on with it, it's your choice, you're an adult, don't open the paper, avoid Ceefax, take control of your life, kick it into touch, don't go to the games, Grow Up.

Ah, if only it was so easy.

And oh.

Oh, how easy it is to give advice.

He's right, though, my friend is right, of course he's right, but what goes on drawing the moths to the flame? Why follow something so unfair, something so likely to hurt you, and so likely to go on hurting you? Because once you're in it, once you know the smell of failure and the long depression and the sudden high and the sudden hit you can feel, it's in your blood and you're an addict. You might get clean for a spell but you're only kidding yourself. You're just one score away from happiness.

So, Mr Seth, you ask me how we helpless fathers deal with the downs. Badly, in my case. Vikram's writing career has been a huge success, but I wonder how you would have felt if Vikram, a young Indian cricketing hero, with posters of him high up everywhere, if young Vikram had strapped on his pads and walked out to the wicket in front of the adoring crowds and taken guard? How well do you handle failure when it can hit you on a daily basis, how do you stay resolute and focused when so much seems stacked up against you? Well, you have to. I could, sitting here over dinner in Delhi, give you the Greeks-to-Beckett line. If they had been born elsewhere, no doubt Aeschylus and Sophocles and Euripides would have been fans who understood the full horrors of the game, because only a Greek cricket follower would write 'we are born to trouble as the sparks fly upward', and Samuel Beckett was a cricketer, no surprises there, because only an Irish cricketer could write 'you must go on, I can't go on, I'll go on', you have no option, you just have to get on with it, we're all born astride the grave, all innings must come to an end, we grow up only to die, all we can do is to keep the ball in play, to play the games of the mind and the body and the spirit and to keep playing and one day it will all be over.

Where's the justice in that?

There isn't any.

It just goes like that.

I can't remember when it didn't.

16

Not watching Ed

Believe it or not, I cannot recall the first time I saw Ed play in a competitive match. He must have been eight or nine. Anyway, he was much the age I was when I first went down the A38 to the county ground at Bristol to see Tom. Or, 'down Bris', as we used to say. In truth, I rarely saw Ed at the crease when he was a young boy because on the days when he was playing in his earliest matches I was either teaching English in my classroom or taking a cricket practice myself.

This was no deprivation. I loved teaching and I enjoyed coaching cricket. I always identified strongly with the class I was teaching or with the team I was running, as I have done with whatever department or school I have been in. 'They' quickly became 'my' team, 'my' department and 'my' school. I have always liked the feeling that I belong to a community: to be a part of something fulfils a part of me. This has not of course ever stopped me being very critical of 'my' team or my anything else. You always hurt the one you love.

You always hurt the one you love.

That was a Mills Brothers song, wasn't it?

Or was it Spike Jones and His City Slickers?

Something tells me Ringo Starr recorded it as well.

And when it all went badly wrong on the sports field did Time lessen the pain? A bit but only a bit. As a schoolboy, and right on into my twenties, I felt dry mouthed and sick for a few hours after any defeat by any team I was in or had coached or was supporting. At its worst I felt humiliated and 'let down', particularly if my team had 'folded' or given up. That was the same if it was Wales in rugby or Kent in cricket (Kent I followed like a fanatic) or Tonbridge School 3rd XI. Over the years that intensity and gloom may have diminished just a little but I would certainly not claim to have grown out of it let alone grown up.

After a bad result for my team or a disappointment for Ed I now only go through about an hour's grumpiness or (as I prefer to see it) 'a quiet spell'.

Perhaps I was secretly relieved about my enforced absence from Ed's earliest matches as my presence on the boundary might only have made him nervous. 'You don't want to put pressure on the boy', as they say. Also, more to the point, I knew I would be very nervous myself watching him bat or bowl, so saying I was teaching in my classroom or entering my course work marks or coaching in the nets not only made me feel hard-working and virtuous but also got me off that particularly searching test of my own character.

I do remember him scoring twenty odd once while I was half-hidden behind an oak tree and unsure which way round the trunk to peer. In this tactic I was apparently in good company. Chris Cowdrey told me that Colin was often to be half-spotted half-hidden behind a tree and Chris claimed that he spent too much time while he was batting trying to establish which tree his famous father was behind when he would have been much better advised keeping his head down and his eye on the ball.

Dealing with winning – as well as telling your children how to behave after winning – is easy. In victory you have to appear to be modest. In victory you should try to eschew or at the very least try to temper your air punching triumphalism, partly because triumphalism is in itself unattractive but mainly because (and we're back to superstition here) if you are a cocky little sod you will suffer a severe stuffing in the very near future because if there is one thing the gods of cricket do like it is rigorously stuffing cocky triumphalist little sods.

So, enjoy your victory to the full in private but do not gloat in public.

That is about all that needs to be said on the best way of

handling success: just 'Enjoy!' as solicitous waiters increasingly tend to say when they hand you your food, and I do wish they wouldn't. We're Brits. We don't go in for all that enjoy stuff.

The other experience, the Big F, requires rather fuller treatment. For a start, there is so much more failure to face in cricket than there is success to enjoy. There is, you might say, so much more to 'f' about. 'All happy families resemble each other', you know Tolstoy's famous opening sentence, and 'each unhappy family is unhappy in its own way', and whether that rings a bell with you or not, there are certainly many more books written about tragedy than about comedy. An awful lot of people do seem to have failed in a quite spectacular way, and to have had those failures memorably recorded.

Just go to the English Faculty Library on any university campus. In the tragedy section the shelves are groaning. There's Aeschylus and Sophocles and Euripides – yes, we're back again to the Greeks – and then there's Marlowe, Shakespeare, Webster, Ibsen and Strindberg, Arthur Miller, and the Irish cricketer Beckett, they're everywhere, the tragedians, and everyone's reading them, you can't get away from every kind of death. In literature as in cricket we seem to home in on doom and gloom. Failure sells like hot cakes.

And every literary critic and every would-be novelist thinks he has a tragic book in him. There are many more words spoken and words printed on unhappiness than happiness, more stories about disaster than the happily-ever-after, so when your children 'fail' or 'have a bad day' it is difficult not to over identify, difficult not to put yourself in their shoes, not to feel their pain, difficult not vicariously to 'go through' whatever purgatory they are going through.

Above all, it is not easy finding the right words to say when you meet up in the car park or behind the pavilion after the game and hordes of the opposition supporters are honking past in full spate. What kind of comfort can you offer the player who failed that day who happens to be your son? How on earth can you manage to be helpful and practical without being critical? How can you be supportive and sympathetic without inviting self-indulgence and encouraging self-pity?

It's a bit like the problem of how much truth do you tell to a friend when you see he is in trouble and he tells you he is in trouble and you know the trouble he is in is partly if not mostly self-inflicted. What do you say? For a start, how sure are you of your own take on the truth, and, even more, how sure are you of your friend's ability to take it?

Sometimes people have told me things, told me much more revealing things than I ever imagined about them, and I have been speechless and out of my depth, but I also know that I have to say something 'helpful' or palliative. And when you have heard them out do you say:

'You shouldn't have done that.'
'Why on earth did you do that?'
'Was that sensible?'
'Well, that wasn't a very good idea, was it?'
'Bit of an error of judgement, wasn't it?'

Or do you, as I do, say:

'That's a difficult one, that is. Blimey. Phew.'
'I need a bit of time to absorb this one.'

If you've won the match, of course, you're bouncing along behind the stands, beaming goodwill on friend and in particular on foe and singing *You're The Best* by Tina Turner, and *You're The Best* is mixing and morphing into a rousing chorus of Bette Midler's *Did you ever know that you're my hero*, so when you meet up with the successful player, and let's say in this immodest instance he is your son, you have a nice range of options and any one of the following could happily tumble out:

'Bloody fan-tastic!'

'How about that!'

'Let's stop for a meal.'

'Tell you what, we don't want to get ahead of ourselves, but I reckon we're going to win everything this year.'

After you lose, however, you're walking slowly towards the pavilion or the car park and not singing anything at all because it is very difficult to sing with a croakingly dry throat and a pain in your churning gut and an ache in your sinking heart and there are no exclamation marks in sight because the person who failed (now showered and changed) is walking towards you and you have to be very cautious indeed over how you start and to choose very carefully one from the menu, one from the following options:

'Oh well.'

'Never mind.'

'It'll turn, it'll turn.'

'It happens, it happens.'

'It's a very cruel old game.'

'Somehow it all felt as if it was never to be.'

'One of those days, eh? Round the next corner.'

'It's still early in the season, plenty of games to go, eh?'

Like any idiot I can of course come up with all the fibre-stiffening stuff about failing, about the Big F being good for your character, and I can talk about the importance of learning to deal with it. I can talk with the best of them about the need to stand on your own two feet, the need to have a good look in the mirror, even to suggest that you might with advantage read the stoic philosophy of Marcus Aurelius:

> Be like the rocky headland on which the waves constantly break. It stands firm, and round it the seething waters are laid to rest.

'It is my bad luck that this has happened to me.' No, you

should rather say: 'It is my good luck that, although this has happened to me, I can bear it without pain, neither crushed by the present nor fearful of the future.' Because such a thing could have happened to any man, but not every man could have borne it without pain…
So in all future events which might induce sadness remember to call on this principle: 'This is no misfortune, but to bear it true to yourself is good fortune.'

Marcus Aurelius, *Meditations*, 4.49
trans. Martin Hammond

Because it's a tough old world out there and you might as well find that out sooner rather than later and be a man, my son, and take it on the chin and come up for more. I can say all that and quote Marcus Aurelius, and I have said all that and quoted Marcus Aurelius, and saying it is one thing but keeping your true feelings out of the expression on your stoical and classically trained face as you quote Marcus Aurelius is quite another.

When I had played particularly badly myself and failed in cricket or rugby, I could hardly look people in the eye. This went for the spectators as well as my team mates. I read it on their faces ('You are a failure, Smith') and I scurried away as quickly as possible, did anything to get in the car, to jump on the bus, to run for the train, go anywhere to get the hell out of it all and as far away as possible from their eyes as they walked towards me.

Anyway.

One September afternoon in 1995, when Ed was eighteen and playing club cricket, he made 183 not out, setting a new batting record for the Kent League, and it was looking likely that his cricket might take him further than school or club level. With all this just around the corner for him, I began to wonder if my own feelings of inadequacy as a sportsman might get in the way of my full enjoyment of his career.

I was, I sensed, nearing the end of the long road from innocence to experience, from being outside the loop to right on the inside track, or from the particular to the very particular. Because all the emotions, the apprehension and tension and pleasure and pain of the father in the stands, intensify tenfold if your son takes to the pitch.

With Ed on the back pages every day, the claw dug itself ever deeper in my gut. It elbowed itself even more into my life. I came to know more and more about the game. Until, bit by bit, I think I knew too much. After a few years of him playing first class cricket I was on both sides of the boundary, and I'm not sure that works.

-Hey, mate?

-Yes?

-That your son out there?

-Yes. Yes it is.

-Thought it was. Looks a bit like you.

17

So, Jonathan, what exactly did you teach me?

I click back into the Seth dinner table. They are talking about careers. Talking about careers is easy. Talking about writing books to writers can, though, be difficult. Most writers – and with good reason – are cagey about their current project. They are economical about what they are up to at any moment, if indeed they are up to anything, because what they are up to is up to them.

As a writer, if you say too much about what is churning away in your semi-conscious mind or beginning to take shape on paper you may well regret it later. On the other hand, if you say too little why bother to say anything at all? Either way you can become over-sensitive to the questioner's response to any answer you care to give, and as you look at the expression on his or her face your belief in your tentative project is usually draining away even as you speak.

But it never stops anyone asking a writer what he is 'on' at the moment. I suppose it is only natural to ask. And I suppose we should be grateful anyone cares enough to enquire.

Some writers are cagey purely because they fear that their ideas and their next project will be stolen. Careless talk may not cost a writer his life but it can cost him his livelihood. I am too free and easy when I talk and I have suffered for it. I know for a fact, ghastly phrase, but I know for a fact that people have nicked my ideas and rushed something out ahead of me and then claimed serendipity. Not that I can prove it.

A writer's financial rewards are so unpredictable and precarious it is, of course, hazardous to see it 'as a career' for money. A teacher's salary is not much but you can live on it, just, and providing you can keep your hands to yourself your job is secure and full of lasting rewards. Influencing generations of young people's lives for (you hope) the better, and enjoying the daily company of clever colleagues, how do you put a price on that?

Vikram is wondering whether you make a bigger contribution in life or derive more satisfaction by being a politician or a Prime Minister or an engineer or a sportsman or a teacher or a writer? Ed and I have touched on all this many times while walking the Cornish coastal paths.

Who is the more fulfilled?

Do we want to change things, *eg* the world? Or just live a good life?

What do you hope to look back on?

Can we make a difference by simply doing well what we want to do?

If so, what is your voice?

What is your territory?

Vikram is now talking to Ed about these matters and I am listening and I am thinking: if you write a book and it reaches let's say ten thousand people, as one of mine might, that is something. I would not claim too much for it but I would claim that ten thousand people is 'something'. One of my Radio Four plays is received by (or reaches) hundreds of thousands of people. The Radio Four listeners may not know I wrote it, and I am sure very few will remember my name when it is read out at the beginning and the end of the broadcast, but I did write it and they did hear it so I did 'reach' them, didn't I?

I would call that 'something'.

Vikram's books have reached millions of people. I haven't a clue how many millions but I would guess it is many. That is many millions of people's lives enriched by reading a very good book by Vikram Seth. That is a kind of power too, and surely a power for the good. But Vikram has noticed my silence and turns to me with an amused expression.

-What exactly did you teach me at Tonbridge, Jonathan? I've been trying to remember.

-Ah.

Ed is grinning at the slowness of my response, but Vikram may simply be trying to tease and draw me in to the conversation. Or he may be suggesting it would be fun to pin down the details of a distant and briefly shared past.

If it is the second I am at an advantage because I always kept a workbook on my classroom desk: a red exercise book for each term, a new exercise book for each of the one hundred and fourteen terms in which I taught English. Every day I made an entry for each lesson. In no sense would these jottings qualify as lessons plans. More often it was only a line or two on what I was up to, a phrase, a reminder, an anticipation, an anxiety, a doubt that I had handled something or someone well, a thought on this or that, or if I was feeling cavalier and unusually content, it might just be a big approving tick. Ticks were rare.

Before I left England on this trip, aware that we would be meeting up with the Seth family, I had checked my workbooks for 1969 and 1970. As well as that tricky passage from *Coriolanus* and the even trickier speeches of Leontes from the first two acts of *The Winter's Tale*, it seems that I taught Vikram some Elizabethan lyrics and selected poems by George Herbert. I also did exercises in practical criticism (taking in a passage of prose or a bit of Browning or an extract from a play and trying to come to grips with it) before getting on to Arthur Hugh Clough. I particularly remember spending a happy few weeks with Vikram on Clough's long poem *Amours de Voyage*.

What's more I can prove this final claim because I still have the nine-sided essay that he wrote on it. Even better, I am delighted to say that at the very top of the first page, in the title of the essay, the young Seth has misspelt 'Amours' as 'Amors'.

I cannot explain why I should still have his essay. It is very odd that I do. I had written my comments at the bottom and

I would have handed it back to him the next time I taught him, a self-discipline I tried my best to observe all my teaching days. Are we saying then that I was sensing the future and gambling that here was someone to follow, a horse to back? That I asked to have his essay back from him with that motive in my mind? Or did I mutter something along the lines that it would be nice if I could borrow his essay for a few days to show it to the other English teachers – the ones I had phoned, the ones who liked to celebrate the success of their pupils – and that I then forgot to return it to him?

Yes, that is the more likely.

Anyway I have it (tucked safely inside the proof copy of *The Golden Gate*, which he gave me) and I am proud to have it and I am certainly not giving it him back now.

In fact, come to think of it, one of the poems I have brought along for Ed to read on our holiday is by Arthur Hugh Clough. It is witty and serious. It is memorable and true. Indeed, it is the sort of thing Vikram might very well have written himself had he lived in the middle of the nineteenth century.

In recent weeks this poem has taken possession of my mind, especially the telling last verse.

18

There is no God

'There is no God,' the wicked saith,
    'And truly it's a blessing,
For what he might have done with us
    It's better only guessing.'

'There is no God,' a youngster thinks,
    'Or really, if there may be,
He surely didn't mean a man
    Always to be a baby.'

'There is no God, or if there is,'
    The tradesman thinks, 'twere funny
If he should take it ill in me
    To make a little money.'

'Whether there be,' the rich man says,
    'It matters very little,
For I and mine, thank somebody,
    Are not in want of victual.'

Some others, also, to themselves
    Who scarce so much as doubt it,
Think there is none, when they are well,
    And do not think about it.

But country folk who live beneath
    The shadow of the steeple;
The parson and the parson's wife,
    And mostly married people;

Youths green and happy in first love,
    So thankful for illusion;
And men caught out in what the world
    Calls guilt, in first confusion;

And almost everyone when age
    Disease, or sorrows strike him,
Inclines to think there is a God,
    Or something very like him.

              Arthur Hugh Clough (1819-1861)

19

The captain who couldn't look

Across the dinner table Ed might look a bit like a younger me
but if we go back to 1960 there's a world of difference.

In the summer of 1960
Hitchcock's *Psycho* opens, starring Anthony Perkins and
Janet Leigh and a shower curtain
Nye Bevan dies
Khrushchev loses his temper a lot
and I read for the first time the poems of Alun Lewis.

What else?

Shocked and captive, I see *Suddenly, Last Summer*, the film
of the play by Tennessee Williams, and I find out what a
frontal lobotomy is, starring Elizabeth Taylor and
Katharine Hepburn and Montgomery Clift.

and

Penguin shelves plans to publish *Lady Chatterley's Lover*.

It is the summer 1960, and by the sound of it, I was beginning
to grow up a bit, but the thing that really stands out is the news
that I was made captain of cricket at school.

I do not think I have ever taken any role more seriously.

When lessons were over for the day and no-one else was
about, my vice-captain and I often went over to the cricket
pavilion for a smoke. Given all the pressure we were under
we definitely felt in need of a crafty drag. More to the point, I
loved the place, I could have slept in there, the whole
atmosphere got me, the smell of it, the look of it, the mower
oil, the stud-scarred floorboards, the warm dusty air, a few
bats, an old swollen cricket ball with a split seam, a bag or two

of sawdust, some bails and stumps on a table (touch one and they all rolled off), crumpled sweaters left in corners, cardboard-stiff old batting gloves – and underpinning the whole space – all the years of schoolboy hope and glory.

Up in the score box, where the scorer did his wagon-wheel charts for each batsman's innings, blue wisps of cigarette smoke would drift out and dissipate in the evening air. Up there in the scorebox no one could touch us. As the pavilion afforded a 360 degree view of the school grounds we could spot any suspicious master a hundred yards off, and while having a contemplative Silk Cut my vice-captain and I would whiten our boots, tighten our studs, and talk strategy: what to do about the opposition, discuss team selection, re-arrange the batting order and, most difficult of all, ponder the problematic field placings for the off spinner.

While we talked I religiously whitened my boots and then my pads. Whatever happened on the pitch, whatever the result on match days, at least I would look a cricketer. If nothing else I would look the part when I crossed the white line and led my men out against the enemy.

In a further anointing, which came close to a baptismal dousing, I smoothed linseed oil on to my bat, even though the blade was already nearly as brown as the ones in the glass display cases in The Long Room at Lord's. Jack Hobbs used this Gunn and Moore bat when he scored 187 against the Australians at Adelaide on the 1911-1912 Ashes tour. Jonathan Smith failed to use this bat when he missed a straight one for 0 against Monmouth School at Brecon in 1957.

Come to think of it, with all that linseed oil soaked into its face, the only thing that stopped my bat becoming heavier by the day was that I scraped the incriminating red marks off the edges with an old razor blade. A razor blade was a vital tool for the cricketer who liked to shave his bat clean.

As captain I took everything that happened on and off the field very personally. If we failed on the pitch I had failed. If

74

someone bowled a bad over I was angry with him but I felt I also had failed as a captain: I should never have put him on to bowl in the first place. If someone on the boundary dropped a skied and crucial catch it was as if I myself had dropped it. A dropped catch on Saturday meant that next week I would insist on an even longer fielding practice; if need be we would practise steeple high catches until our hands hurt.

After all, the buck stopped with the skipper and who was the skipper? I looked up at the team boards and at the rows of old photographs in the dressing room. There were some big names up there, some Welsh heroes, and that's where I would soon be, first name on the 1960 list and a captain for all time.

My behaviour was out of all proportion. For sport to be fun of course you have to take it seriously but nobody had told me that if you take it too seriously, if you become embattled and beleaguered, it ceases to be any kind of fun at all, and what's more to the point you are likely to play worse. At the time it seemed normal to be obsessed, normal that I thought more about the alternative field placings for the off spinner than I did about the intellectual panache of the Metaphysical Poets and the major battles of Marlborough's campaign (1704-1709).

The thing was I badly wanted to be good at history. More than that I also badly wanted to be good at English, to be a literary historian and an English specialist who could read Latin and Greek literature in the original, who could compare Virgil and Milton, yet the real battles in my head were taking place not on the fields of Trasimene where Mars did mate the Carthaginians but out in the middle, out on the square on Saturdays. Those were the battles I most wanted to win. I hated losing, and if we lost I tended to spiral down very quickly indeed, and when I was down I tended to stay down.

So, nearly fifty years have passed since then and not a lot has changed.

Though I would like to believe otherwise, the more of this I write the more it strikes me that I have not learnt very much in my life. Or perhaps I am learning that I have not learnt. Rather than changing or improving as the years pass it seems I have just got more so. A cricket coach once told me that when he umpired thirty-seven-year-olds he found that they were still making the same stupid mistakes they used to make when they were schoolboys of seventeen.

Or is it that one lives and learns and dies a fool? Whatever, I am still struggling to handle my emotions and to temper my criticism, and despite the best advice of my friends I am still beating myself up emotionally and I am still reading the sports pages before I turn to the leaders or the book reviews. Politics and the arts, important though they are to me, have to wait their turn. And, on those bleak occasions in the early hours of the morning when I am desperate for help, I am still 'praying' in the wrong way.

There was nothing occasional, however, about my praying in the summer of 1960. That summer I prayed a lot. I prayed a lot in chapel, the beautiful chapel at Christ College, which dates from the thirteenth century, and I prayed a lot in my bed.

Poor old God: if he was up there and feeling anything, he must have felt under siege. I tried every kind of earnest entreaty and humble supplication. I tried every tone of voice. I tried to wait on Him when His attention might justifiably have been elsewhere. After all a cricket field in mid Wales was unlikely to make it on to His long list let alone His short list but if He would deliver I promised clear proof of abstinence. He would know what I was referring to.

It didn't work. Nothing worked. I now realize that I was unbalanced if not mad but I did not see it at the time, and anyway it's all relative because I was nowhere near as mad as the boy two beds along in my dormitory who was dedicating his whole life to being Ken Mackay.

OK, you may need to be a fan and a follower of a certain age to know who Ken Mackay is (or, sadly, was as he died far too young). K D 'Slasher' Mackay (1925-1982) was a dour Australian left handed batsman and right arm bowler who came from Queensland, and his nickname was ironic (as cricketer's nicknames tend to be) because the one thing that Ken Mackay was not was a slasher. Ken was laconic and obdurate, indeed unendurably so. While others may have favoured a Sobers high back-lift and free-flowing bat swing, Slasher barely moved his bat out of the blockhole. Slasher went on chewing and bored the bowlers off. He made Trevor Bailey look like a tearaway.

Anyway, having fallen hook line and sinker for Slasher, this boy felt he had to go through exactly what his hero went through, and he thought it best to make a start with the climate. Because it was hot and sticky in the sub-tropical Queensland summer this boy decided that during our cold and wet Welsh winter it was only right and proper to sleep with no pyjamas on and covered only by a sheet. And during our summer, because it was winter in Australia, he had spare blankets piled high on top of his bed. He even asked me to crown it all with my dressing gown. He had that empathy that GCSE examiners are looking for. You could say that he identified.

And if that was not empathy enough he went further, much further. He himself was a natural right handed batsman but one day he changed to being left handed because, well, because Slasher batted left handed. He was always padded up first in the nets and he spent hours practising batting the wrong way round.

Batting the right way round is hard enough for most of us at the best of times but this madman tried to deflect the ball off his body as Slasher would, only to miss it altogether and be hit on the body and on the hands. But such physical pain only called for a bit more impassive chewing. Whatever the punishment he took on the body he just went on chewing as Slasher would have done, and when the big moment came in the match and it was his turn to bat he made his way to the wicket with the lugubrious lope that Ken Mackay had, bending his knees a little as he walked (as Slasher did), took guard left handed, surveyed the field and was strafed.

Sometimes he managed to survive a few balls before the inevitable happened and then he would trudge back to the pavilion in much the way that Slasher might have done (but much earlier).

Some of our matches, I have to admit, were not that Big, *eg* the early season fixture against the Monmouthshire Clergy. Even if you were a cricket mad Low Church Welshman, and there weren't many of those, you would not call the warm-up game against the Monmouthshire Clergy a Big One. These amiable clerics always arrived in old cars and always arrived late, or late enough (we suspected) to cut down the time we had in which to beat them. They sweated a lot when they ran between the wickets, and they panted a lot and they chortled a lot. The Revd F Secombe, Harry Secombe's brother, was in the team – and they certainly tucked into their teas.

When faced by any triumph or disaster on the field of play (and the literary part of me rather liked this) it was their droll custom to come up with an appropriate biblical text. *eg*, when they met us:

'What are these that are arrayed in white robes?'

Or, on being run out:

'What is this that thou hast done?'

Or, after a bad LBW decision:

'My punishment is greater than I can bear.'

And I have just checked the 1960 school magazine and the Monmouthshire Clergy batting card for the 7th May includes this dismissal:

The Archbishop of Wales c Harding b Smith 3

A few of our matches were, however, Big. Those against Cardiff High School and Monmouth School were definitely Big, but the biggest of them all was the match against our deadly rivals, Llandovery College. That year, in the summer of 1960, it was played at their ground on a very hot day.

We fielded first and we fielded poorly (so much for my brutally long fielding practices) and in chasing 184 to win we collapsed to 120-8, and part of the reason for that unnecessary collapse was this statistic:

J B Smith b O'Brien 22

The captain was out attempting to sweep the leg spinner, as I had been a number of times before, and ever since that day I have always considered sweeping leg spinners completely beyond the pale, and as a coach I always reserved my severest rebuke for any batsman who dared to play the shot that I played so badly and so often as a boy. That's growing up for you.

Anyway, when I was out sweeping all seemed lost, and I saw with sickening clarity that it was my fault, all my fault. With a wet towel over my head and with the knife turning slowly in my gut I knew that my name would be up on the boards in the home dressing room, and it would indeed be the first name on the list, but that it would be the name of a losing captain.

Then a minute passed. And another minute passed. I could hear the groans and the roars and the appeals, a near miss or a close run thing, over after over, the sound of bat on ball, of strangled cries, until it seemed as if Thomas and Hancock, our numbers seven and ten, had dug deep and might hold out until the close of play.

Llandovery College tried everything in the book. Minute by minute and over by over they tried everything, by hook and by crook (and I had my suspicions about that lot), and the appeals came faster and thicker and louder, but we somehow got through another over and another over and don't ask me how but we escaped with a draw.

After the final ball had been safely played (we finished on 147-8) I ran down the pavilion steps, a relieved non-losing captain, to shake the hands of our two batsmen (their eyes blazing bright) and the hands of the opposition (their eyes burning low). The relief I felt was deep. It felt so deep I could almost have been a winning captain. Either way, you could call it a draw but we had stuffed Llandovery and you could see it in their eyes.

What I did not admit to anyone, and have not fully admitted to myself until I started to write the last paragraph, was that I had been unable to watch the final hour of that dramatic draw. Throughout that interminable and brave resistance I was sitting facing the pitch, but with my eyes closed.

What would Mike Agassi have made of me?

****

Is there a tendency in followers – no, that is an evasion – is there a tendency in *me* not to face up fully to reality, to face the pitch but to close my eyes, to see and not to see life, or is this just a silly and trivial sporting thing? Sport all matters far more than it should, but what if it comes uncomfortably close to mattering more than anything? I can often take a blow to my own life better than I can take a blow to my team's or to Ed's.

Perhaps my mistake is to think that the people I am following are feeling what I am feeling. They are not. I am sitting there and suffering and imagining that they are going through what I am going through and of course they are not going through it in the same way at all because if they were they would not be able to play, they would not be able to perform. They would go nuts.

They would end up like me.

On a number of occasions I have tried to cut through all this with a cheese wire, to turn over a new leaf, to sort it out blah

blah. In some ways it's not at all unlike trying to get off the drink. I have tried displacement therapy. I have taken the pledge and made the vow.

What I do is I promise myself a small, iced tonic water instead of a large whisky, a glass of sparkling water instead of my favourite claret, and instead of checking the cricket scores on Ceefax or the internet I will read a short story by Chekhov or Anita Desai, something set in Russia or in India, or I will go to see a French film in the afternoon, and after the film I am Robert Louis Stevenson canoeing in Northern France or I am Edward Thomas and set off for a walk, I have walked out in rain and back in rain, and somehow or other I get right through until bedtime and expect to wake up clean the next day.

There have been minor victories, but I know deep down that I can't kick cricket any more than I can the drink. I can't change it because it is me.

I am a dependent.

20

John Inverarity

Mind you, as with all dependents, there have been some ups.

For example?

Well, how about meeting Don Bradman?

In February 1982 my agent rang me to say that BBC Television wanted to make a four part serial of my first novel, *Wilfred and Eileen*.

Was that OK by me?

They were only paying £x.

Would £x be all right?

Should she sign?

Yes, I said to my agent, that was OK by me, yes indeed, that was all right by me, she should sign, in fact she should snap their hand off before they changed their minds. I wasn't proud, £x was a whole lot better than £0, and as soon as the cheque was nestling in my bank account I went straight down to the nearest travel agent and bought four return tickets to Australia.

Gillie and I, with our baby daughter Becky, had lived for a year in Melbourne in 1974, and I vowed to myself that if we ever could afford it, if ever we had a bit extra, we would return. That wistful hope, as well as the Australian thread in our lives, had been strengthened in 1976 when John Inverarity, the test cricketer, joined the mathematics department at Tonbridge School, and another big influence started to flow into my life.

John Inverarity and I hit it off straight away: talking about teaching, talking cricket technique and talking about our children. Talking anything really. He enjoyed being in England as much as I enjoyed being in Australia. We loved the similarities and the differences between our countries, and we also shared a loathing of all the 'professional' insider mysteries in education and sport that could and should be simply expressed. Above all, we both hated educational jargon, especially that employed on In Service Training days.

At one such training day – with a short coffee break for screaming – we were being lectured (with handouts and overhead projection) on the need to bring 'differentiation' into our lessons. And in case we had missed it, 'differentiation' was all up there on the big screen for, oh I don't know, a couple of hours:

- *differentiation* by classroom organization is a way of helping pupils to access knowledge, increase understanding, develop concepts and practise skills.
- *differentiation* by paired task is a way of helping pupils to self-assess, peer assess, target set and practise skills to reach targets.
- *differentiation* by outcome is a way of both accessing knowledge and experiences and assessing at the end of the teach and practise cycle.

Reading or listening to such stuff makes me want to start a brawl there and then. Part of me wants a rant. Part of me wants to stand up and point and shout hey, tell you what, I've got something here, and it's a bit better than what's up there on the screen, and tell you what, it was written in 1580 by a bloke called Montaigne, Michel de Montaigne, so why don't you all write this down instead:

If the teachers undertake to regulate many minds of such different capacities and forms with the same lesson and a similar measure of guidance, it is no wonder if in the whole race of children they find barely two or three who reap any proper benefit from their teaching.

Montaigne, 1580

But I never do shout such things out. Instead I usually sit

there and seethe and try to block it all out with a fantasy, and the usual one usually works. Right, you're in the car, you're driving west, windows down, music on, and she's next to you...

Or, if that fails, if she fails to turn up, if that one doesn't work, I try to cheer myself up by silently reciting something gloomy, a poem or a passage of prose, something laugh-out-loud bleak, say, my favourite bit of Beckett, my favourite bit from the left-handed Irish cricketer, that bit from *Watt*, how does it go, how does it run...

The Tuesday scowls, the Wednesday growls, the Thursday curses, the Friday howls, the Saturday snores, the Sunday yawns, the Monday mourns, the Monday morns. The whacks, the moans, the cracks, the groans, the welts, the squeaks, the belts, the shrieks, the pricks, the prayers, the kicks, the tears, the skelps, and the yelps.

I felt a firm nudge on my elbow. John handed me a note.
-Fancy a net?

****

When John Inverarity could not find anyone better he would ask me to bowl at him. I was, of course, cannon fodder: a helpful Pom asking to be smashed. He smiled at the speed of my run up, he licked his lips as my arm came over and he beamed at what came out of my hand; and before I walked off into rural Kent to retrieve the balls he wondered if I might be able to run in and bend my back and put a little bit more into it. I told him I was putting a great deal into it, thank you, and my back was quite bent enough already.

Anyway, in July 1982, thanks to my novel *Wilfred and Eileen*, the Smiths – and this time there were four of us, one clutching a small cricket bat – were going back to Australia. It meant we would miss out on a whole summer holiday watching Kent, following Kent home and away, and in particular following

Chris Cowdrey, but we would instead be able to re-visit all our old friends in Melbourne and then stay with our new friends, the Inverarities, who were living in Adelaide.

R J Inverarity, often called 'Invers' in cricketing circles, played six tests for Australia. When he retired after twenty three years in the first class game, he had scored more runs in the Sheffield Shield than any other batsman in its history. He was a brilliant leader, a fine top order batsman, an orthodox left arm spinner and a superb slip catcher. Even more significantly, he captained Western Australia and led them to four Sheffield Shield triumphs in five years. In later spells as a coach in England John Inverarity dramatically improved Kent's performance, and while he was at Warwickshire they won the County Championship in 2004.

As a captain Invers has often been seen as the Australian equivalent of Mike Brearley. There is considerable sense in this comparison. Brearley was in charge when Middlesex won four county championships and under him England won seventeen tests and lost only four. In fact Brearley and I were undergraduates together at St John's College, Cambridge, in the same years (1960-64) – he read classics and then philosophy – and I knew him a little.

Any side led into the field by Brearley or Inverarity had an advantage even before the umpire called 'Play' and the first ball was bowled. It's not that they were clever. Of course they were clever. And of course they were leaders. But there are a lot of clever men and women all over the place misleading people in all kinds of daft directions, and I can think of one county cricket captain who acted as if the more unfathomable and bizarre his field placings and declarations were the more clever he would seem and the more he would bamboozle the opposition. All he ended up being was more wrong.

No, it's not the cleverness about Brearley and Inverarity that mattered, it's that they were shrewd, analytical, intuitive and perceptive. Both instinctively understood how to make a team more than the sum of its parts. While loving the 'engagement' and the heat of the battle, and while enjoying the respect and even the devotion of their players, they also knew how to assess and, if need be, how to stand apart. Brearley, not surprisingly, has since become a practising psychoanalyst and Inverarity a famous leader in education.

Captaining a cricket team at the highest level is possibly the toughest leadership role in sport but what Inverarity did in cricket he later did for his staff and his pupils as the Headmaster of Hale School in Perth, and then again at the University of Western Australia. I spent some time teaching in Perth and I saw him at work. Whether it was in the sporting arena or in the wider life of the school, he revealed the same approach, the same mindset and the same beliefs; and those he led with such success in those different worlds recognized this. They recognized him and they honoured him. There is the John Inverarity Stand at the WACA ground in Perth, and the new Music and Arts Centre at Hale School is named after him. Each world, I am convinced, benefited from his involvement with the other.

How did he do it?

What was his special chemistry?

What were his gifts as a captain and as a Headmaster?

In his manner around the school campus John Inverarity had (let's get the Montaigne quotes out of the way in this chapter) a touch of what the French essayist memorably called 'severe gentleness'. There was kindness but there was toughness, there was understanding but there was expectation. He listened to teachers and to pupils and to parents in an absorbed way, and then sifted it. Getting it right is, I suspect, partly based on listening and on getting to know people, but miles away from trying to please everyone or going along with whatever the last person said to you.

Nor did John Inverarity sit bunkered in his office, as so many Heads now prefer to do, surrounding themselves with an ever growing secretariat and an ever growing senior management team and an ever growing obsession with computer screens and process and statistics and relying on the Maginot Line of emails. No, he got out and about and looked hard and straight at the world as it is, with hope, and certainly with a measure of idealism, but with clear eyes.

John based his leadership moves on experience, on a record of proven success, and on a balanced assessment of the likely developments. The first thing he wanted to know about any cricketer was what had he done so far, how many runs had he scored, how many wickets had he taken, what had his career to date showed. A person's past, in other words, was the best indicator of his future. It was the same with teachers. He did not rush to make dramatic or smart-arsed or eye-catching statements or appointments, nor did he swim with the tide, yet what he said often stood up to the daily buffetings of reality.

How can one man make such a telling difference? Well, forget cricket for a moment, and forget chalky teachers: he had most of the qualities required for leadership in any walk of life, but there were three in particular which I believe are rarely to be found in one person:

- judgement
- a fusion of coolness and passion
- and a deep interest in developing the lives of others.

There was also, I have to admit, a small silly coincidence in John Inverarity's career that caught my eye early on, a detail that not only privately pleased me but seemed to be a promising sign. On 25th July 1968, a full eight years before I first met him, John was playing for Australia against England in the Headingley Test match, and that was the only time that Tom Graveney captained England, and Tom Graveney was only captaining England on that occasion because Colin Cowdrey was ill.

You may say it is 'only sport' but I felt that some of the random dots in my life were joining up to make a pattern – Graveney, Cowdrey, Brearley, Inverarity – and the pattern went far beyond cricket.

21

Tea with a ledge

Legends, like myths, used to be things of the past: the myths and legends and sagas of Ancient Greece and Rome, classical stories and stormy sea passages and fabulous beasts merging into medieval courts, exaggerated or idealized conceptions, things we looked back on through the mists of time. That was how legends were. But to be a legend now you don't have to be dead; in fact, legends are very much alive and fairly thick on the ground, just look around you, just listen in on the Tube or in a bar or (perforce) to the motormouth on his mobile:

'Hi, Legend, good to see you!'
'Legend, great to hear you!'
'He-e-e-e-y, Leg-end!'

Or, at a push, just 'leg' will do, as long as it is pronounced 'ledge'. And the great thing is, and when you come to think of it, this is what is so great about our country, that we can all be legends, know what I mean, we're now all legends, legends in our own lifetime, the barman who serves you a drink after hours is a legend, the bloke who gives you his unexpired parking ticket is a legend, the guy who lends you his bedroom so that you can settle in there for the weekend with your girl friend is a 'ledge', well obviously he is. I heard someone recently called 'ledge' for getting his tax return in on time.

Don Bradman, who I think we can all agree was a 'ledge', toured this country for the fourth and last time in 1948, which was just before I tuned in to the game. In 1948 I was in my second year in primary school and I was into conkers and hide-and-seek and avoiding the playground bully. I had not yet held a cricket bat or bowled a ball. So, apart from a few black and white shots of The Don on film, I never saw him play the game, and I did not know until recently that he considered that his side's victory at Leeds in 1948, when Australia made 404 in the fourth innings to win, with Bradman himself walking off the field with 173 not out, was the pinnacle of his career. Eric Scarbrough, my father-in-law, saw that innings.

When the Smiths went to stay with the Inverarities in Adelaide in 1982 they lived at 6 Holden Street, Adelaide. Sir Donald and Lady Bradman lived next door but one at 2 Holden Street.

Invers and I were both teaching in school every day of the week, but one Sunday the Bradmans came round for afternoon tea. Ed (five years old a few days earlier) was hugging his new S S bat in both arms as they walked in. The Don signed it on the back, a signature which became fainter and fainter in the years following as the bat was exposed to relentless practice in the sun and the wind and the rain. Chipped and battered and split and dark brown, with its rubber grip perished, the bat is still here but the most famous of sporting autographs has now disappeared. It was there but now it has gone.

Yet somehow that feels completely natural and right to me, time passes, the rain runs down the signed names on cricket bats as well as on the carved gravestones, an anecdote fit for Thomas Hardy:

Ah, no: the years, the years;
Down their carved names the rain-drop ploughs.

It was a surprise, of course it was, when Bradman first walked in. All the family, Gillie, me, Becky and Ed, took it in turns to shake his hand. Could this serene man really have punished bowlers the world over and dominated test match cricket for twenty years? Was this man shaking our hands the legend, the master who bestrode the game from 1928 to 1948?

We sat there in a circle eating cakes and listening to the greatest cricketer who ever lived – the greatest sportsman who ever lived – field our questions, questions that must have been put to him ten thousand times, and it does not matter now what his answers were, and I can't even remember:

Who was the quickest bowler he faced?
Who was the best leg spinner he had seen?
Why did fast bowlers break down so often now?
What should be done about the ever slower over rates?
What should be done about excessive use of the bouncer?
What did he think of night cricket/coloured clothing/white balls?

Or have I imagined that last question? Was all that already happening in 1982? Anyway, we drifted out to the back garden and John Inverarity threw/bowled some balls at Ed and Bradman watched.

Later that week we walked to the centre wicket at the Adelaide Oval – this was July and the Australian winter so the ground was deserted – the ground where the infamous body line attack on Bradman took place in 1934 and where, in later days, Colin Cowdrey made his highest first class score, 307, against South Australia in 1962. And who, in that match, was Colin's partner in a stand of 344? T W Graveney.

We glanced round at the stands and at the cathedral. I looked down the pitch and drew a deep breath and Ray Lindwall was running in and I was right there, I was Tom Graveney again, the crowd was roaring abuse, my sleeves were rolled up to just below the elbow, my shirt was sticking to my back, and I was licking the salt off my lips and very determined to shut up all the Aussies baying for my blood.

What on earth was I up to?

It was my five year old son who should be going through all this. Why does all this stuff still mean so much to me? I wish it didn't. Even when I try to trace the journey and attempt to join up the dots it still seems a slow burn which became a kind of madness. Nor do I know where such an obsession takes root, or where the desire to succeed in it begins to take hold.

There was never any purpose on our part, certainly for many years, to see Ed play cricket at a 'serious' level. I can't speak for him but all through his school days I never considered it. I think perhaps his sister Becky was the one of us who knew just how much he wanted it. But professional sport seemed to me then – and still seems to me now – the most precarious of trades.

But as his parents we were (and we are) in a sense responsible for his life. We gave him books to read and we talked and we analysed everything and we were his bowling machine. No doubt some people, watching me in the nets with my jacket off, doing throw-downs in the evening, thought I was yet another father trying to turn his son into the player he himself never was. Perhaps I was.

Whatever, we took him to all those Kent games, to see Knott and Underwood, to see Ellison and Cowdrey, and on 1st September 1984, two years after meeting Bradman in Adelaide, we took him to his first Nat West Cup Final at Lord's.

22

Down to the last ball

Although I wrote about the match at the time, looking back at that distant September I find many of the details have slipped away. Even the names of some of the players, rightly famous in their day, now take a while to flicker and return.

Though much may have evaporated or gone fuzzy at the edges, I can however still bring back to the screen a few things. I can, for example, feel again the special anticipation inside Lord's, that Big Day buzz just before the first ball is bowled. Then I see a quick snapshot of Becky and Ed fighting over the binoculars as Chris walks out to bat. And, of course, I could never forget the decisive – the appalling – thrill of the very last delivery, with so much hanging on it.

As for the overall emotional clutch of the occasion, that has, if anything, tightened over the years. Though we would never for a moment have dreamt it would turn out like this, the two counties pitted against each other on 1st September 1984 were the two counties that Ed would, when he grew up, play for: Kent and Middlesex.

(i) Before the first ball.

> 'Excuse me, thanks. Sorry. Excuse me, thanks. Sorry.'
> 'Right, we've made it, these are our seats.'

I was carrying a big bottle of lemonade, a pack of Mars bars, a pack of Penguins, cheese and ham doorsteps wrapped in greaseproof paper, Cokes, apples and bananas, two daily papers, a pair of binoculars, sun hats (you never know), ice bags and a few beers. The usual stuff then.

The children, as far as I can recall, were carrying a biro each. Unlike the half empty Lord's finals of recent years, there was not a spare seat to be seen. I look round at the mass settling. Fans hail each other with thumbs up of recognition, lowering carrier bags, people from every walk of life and in every kind of dress. I can see T-shirts, lightweight jackets, a Kent tie, the loud, the surly, the young and old, a battered Panama hat, some shirts straining at their buttons, some shirts undone, an Army battle jacket, jeans, a Middlesex tie, blazers, anoraks, beer guts and banter, plus the obligatory loner with his big score book open on his knees and his four different colour pens poised for action.

I look over to the pavilion, then up at the Kent balcony, hung with hops, wondering what it must be like to be a player, hoping he will perform, hoping against hope that it will be his day. The umpires are coming out.

Next to me, Ed is nervously clicking his biro.

(ii) Before the last ball.

After eight hours of cricket the scores are level.

And this last ball has to be faced. In both senses.

After 120 overs (less one ball) the scores are the same.

Kent made 232-6 in their innings, with Chris top-scoring with 58, including swatting Wayne Daniel into the Mound Stand for six. Middlesex are now also on 232-6. So one good ball, one good shot, will decide it. Or one bad ball, one bad shot. Nerves are at full stretch out there on the pitch and they're at full stretch up here in the stands. Not a cork is popping; not a can is cracking.

Ed, eyes intense, is beside himself. Beside him I am beside myself. If Middlesex score off the last ball, they've won. If Kent stop them scoring off the last ball Kent have won on a faster scoring rate in the early overs.

It's all down to this ball.

All we want is a dot ball.

Something unplayable would be nice.

No pressure then, Richard Ellison.

We know Richard Ellison. This is personal.

What is he feeling?

He is at the end of his run up.

'Come on, Rich,' Ed screams.

Ellison starts to run in, it is Ellison to Emburey, fine cricketer to fine cricketer, and anything can happen. The arm comes over. Emburey hits it. Where did it go? A bit late, I pick it up, a dark red flash. It goes past square leg. It goes for four.

But oh, where did my heart go?

We sag. The players dash for the pavilion. We slump in our seats. A man, a Middlesex man, is screaming with joy, bawling into my right ear. Over-doing it a bit, isn't he? Turn it down, mate. We are staring, staring speechlessly at the pitch. What went wrong?

'What happened, Dad?'

Don't ask me.

It's all so unfair, all this winners and losers stuff.

And don't let anyone, *any*-one, tell me that Middlesex wanted it more than Kent did.

Say anything but don't say that.

Because it's tripe.

You can't want it more than we did.

In fact you can want it too much.

But you can't always get what you want.

'You can't always get what you want.'

Rolling Stones, 1969.

Let it Bleed album.

Gillie, head down, starts slowly to pack up our bags.

'That's what it's all about,' someone behind me says sadly, crumpling a beer can.

It's over, lads, it's all over. And that includes all the if-onlies as well, it's all written down in the score book, look in the papers tomorrow.

We are soon among the thousands who are moving across the ground to watch the presentations up on the pavilion balcony. This was, you may recall, in the days when the fans were trusted to walk on the grass. For a second I did, I admit, consider grabbing all our stuff and dashing for the Tube, to join the crowd funnelling past the mounted police and up Wellington Road, but we're not exactly in a dashing mood, and it does seem a bit of a cheat to run away now, to desert your side just because they lost, because nobody let anyone down, did they?

Yes, OK, we lost and it's sad but you do need a settling period, a coming to terms period, because in a sense we Smiths are part of the wider team, and it's a bit like that moment in the theatre straight after the hero's death and just before the final curtain, it's like the last thirty lines or so of a Shakespeare play, when the hero is dead, he's very dead, he's lying there on the stage, and others are dead too because somehow or other they got caught up in his life, whether guilty or guiltless they're part of the collateral damage, heroes and villains, goners alike, and while it is a condign punishment for some of the corpses for others it is unjust, but the main thing is it's all over, it's finished, and you can't reverse or rewind anything, and the beauty of it is that you are alive and you were there, a part of it, they fought their fight out in public and they did what they did and this is not the time to point fingers, this is not the time to pass judgement. This is the time to pay your respects and to say the appropriate things.

Ed was, though, inconsolable.

Look, it's not the First World War, is it? It's not the trenches.

And there was a happy ending: a few days after the final Chris Cowdrey was selected for the England tour party. In the winter of 1984/85 he would be in India.

23

Believing

Lead me from falsehood to truth, from darkness to light, from death to immortality.

We pass between the two stone elephants and climb up the steep steps. Just inside the temple – the entrance of a Hindu temple faces east – there are eight or ten women sitting on the floor in what seems like a loose communal circle. They move or play with flowers on the stone floor, or re-arrange them by sensitive brush strokes, their strong practical hands touching small flowers about the size of daisies. They handle the flowers in a natural yet somehow sacred way. They lean forward, their hands still subtly changing the configuration of the flowers, attentive to each other and with some shared purpose, their heads quite close together. They are either communing quietly or praying, or might it just be the softest of chanting?

In another culture and another context these women could well be taken for gossips. I cannot tell what is going on and it feels rude to peer. This is a new form of religious congregation for me, if congregation is the word. Everything here in India feels old and new.

Apart from visiting a suburban temple (previously a community hall) on a school trip to Coventry in 1997, the Jagdish Temple in Udaipur (built 1630-50) was the first Hindu place of worship I had entered. It is a beautiful and affecting place. To reach it we walked past the palace and down through the bazaars where I handled and nearly bought a leather bound notebook only to decide that my suitcase was too heavy as it is, and anyway I already have enough writing paper.

I knew that Hindus venerated an array of deities, possibly thousands of them, but I knew little more than that. Our guide tells me that most temples are, however, dedicated to a presiding deity, in this case Vishnu, and that I should move a little closer to the statue, in front of which a gathering of men and women are singing mantras and other devotional songs. There are fifteen or so worshippers standing there. At the end, I am told, as a concluding ritual, there will be water sprinkled over them.

Occasionally a big drum is banged.

My eye wanders.

There are friezes and four smaller shrines. They are dedicated, our guide whispers, to Lord Ganesh, Shiva, the Sun God and Goddess Shakti. On one level I am at a loss and already nodding on information overload but I am held by it all. Furthermore, and it is hard to look and hard not to look, one of the men worshipping is disfigured in a way I have never witnessed. Hanging from the right side of his face is a fold of skin as large and heavy and long as the inner tube of a rugby ball. It could be the ear of a baby elephant. He is singing.

I look away.

On our way to the temple it was clear that our guide was the most devout of men, and he often turned to me in the course of our days together and said,

-We believe in many things, sir.

He smiles each time he says this, and I smile too. He says it with a smile but openly, as a simple matter of fact. It is a statement expressed with no defensiveness and certainly couched in no irony. We believe in many things, sir, no question. He does not ask me what I believe in but the question is hanging there between us. I suspect he suspects that I am a ...

Well, what on earth do I believe in?

I would not know how to explain my position, if I even have one that merits the name, so I ask him about the gathering of women. He says they meet there, and in much the same way, every morning. It is a central part of their day, a part of their life. They have always been there; they would always be there. More than that he could not say.

Having answered my questions he keeps on checking if I wish to rest. He is most solicitous on this issue, suggesting that I do not over-do it in the heat. In fact the temperature outside is ideal, the high seventies, a clear sunny day of clean air – perfect for a game of cricket – and inside the temple it is cool, so I suspect Ed has said something about me to him.

After the sprinkling of the water, we slowly move away and then slowly go back down the steep steps and between the stone elephants. The disfigured man is now on my right so that I can only see his normal side. The guide again urges me to be careful with the steps. They are worn so smooth from centuries of feet that they are slippery, he says, and I could fall. If this was England he'd be busy filling in his Risk Assessment Form.

If I rub the cornerstone of the stairwell seven times, he tells me, and it must be seven, it will bring me luck. Now that is the kind of thing I do take very seriously and he is pleased that I start rubbing straightaway. At the bottom of the temple steps he picks up some rice grains from a small bowl and he silently wishes. He tells me if there is an odd number of grains between his fingers his wish will come true. He counts them out for me, looks up and opens his hand and laughs. The number is even.

-We believe in many things, sir. Please sit down now. You look tired.

I am not at all tired so he and I wander around the outside walls while Ed goes round the other way to take some photographs. We look up at the spire, then at the ornate carvings depicting moments from the life of Krishna, as well as sculpted dancers, horsemen, elephants, monkeys and musicians. The elephants are for luck. There are some explicit erotic scenes.

I liked being in Udaipur – the water, the lake, the mountains (in the distance it could be Andalusia), this temple – it's the Indian city I have felt most at ease in. And above all I liked being with this gentle Indian. Mind you, I have not yet met a domineering or uncivil Indian. I know we are only scratching the surface of this country, and I know that we are tourists spoilt beyond belief, but there must be some domineering or uncivil Indians surely? Or are the Smiths not allowed to meet them?

Our guide says he is enjoying the days with us because it is good to see a father and a son on a holiday together. He tells me I am lucky to have a son and a son who is a cricketer. I tell him that I know that I am lucky. It would indeed be grotesque for me to complain about anything. We are staying in the Lake Palace Hotel, a fairytale spot, a hotel floating on a lake, and they tell me it was the setting for the James Bond movie *Octopussy* as well as for Paul Scott's *Jewel in the Crown*, the superb TV series I watched in 1984.

The lake is Lake Pichola. The water laps against the wall of our bedroom and because of the last monsoon season there is plenty of it. Ferries and gondolas pass my window. A few hundred yards across the water are the high walls of the City Palace. It is Venice in Rajasthan.

In the central courtyard of the filmic hotel there are cool spreading trees under which I sit and read. Or surreptitiously write bits of this in my notebook. Every fifteen minutes or so a man comes out to tug a piece of string, which rings a tree-top bell to scare the birds out of the branches overhead. This is to stop them evacuating onto the guests (well, me mainly) and onto the polished marble terrace. The success rate of this tactic is patchy, a tactic repeated in a different guise around the swimming pool where an attendant stands with a wide broom and a cloth and no sooner does the pigeon splat than the attendant sweeps, scoops and wipes.

'Self denying, that's us,' Ed says, dark glasses on, lying back on his towel at the side of the pool. He suggests we have a vodka and tonic, only he pronounces it 'wodka', which sets us off, and we wonder which wegetables we shall have at dinner. He has his wodka, I have my Assam tea. After a pause I tell him that earlier in the day I saw a wulture, well two wultures, flying high above the palace. The birds of India, what a bonus they have been: kites, vultures, hawks, swifts, hoopoes, and all the colourful ones I have never seen – even in a book – and cannot name.

No, as well as being silly I am lucky to be in India, I am clear about that.

****

Before I go to sleep each night, when things are still and the only sounds I can hear are my own shallow breathing and the water lapping, I talk to myself about my mother and my father. I try – and sometimes it takes me a while – to bring their faces in front of me, to summon them back. I am determined that my memories of my parents will not be dominated by images of their final years, when the indignities came to stay and when I could and should have been more tolerant. All that is beyond repair now and I would rather re-live and celebrate happier moments. So I think of them and I go on thinking of them until they do appear.

It could be them on any day or at any stage of their lives. I don't mind. The precise form of their re-appearance is not of my choosing. I do not know what is going to occur until, in my father's case, I can feel his hand. As soon as that physical presence happens, I can see him kneeling in the vegetable patch among the runner beans and the broad beans and the peas. He's in his braces and his worn corduroy trousers, always corduroy, his gardening trousers in fact, and he has caught the sun on his face. He's as brown as a berry, as brown as the nutmeg on Mum's rice pudding.

And, with my father, his 'hand' is the right memorial. He had, in the old-fashioned use of the term, a good hand, that is,

101

his handwriting, his penmanship was distinctive and clear. My own illegible handwriting is now a family joke and a trial to my friends but I sit down to write each day in the belief that the words we put down on paper can 'touch' the reader in the way nothing else can, with a touch as powerful as the physical, and with a reach far beyond the tangible. Though reticent to a fault – he never spells out such things – Wordsworth, more than any writer I know, has this sense of a compassionate touch, as if your hand is in his as you walk through life.

Now for my mother.

Her arms all suds in the sink, she's up to her elbows in the family wash, or she is baking a damson tart over a hot oven, and I am racing to the sweet shop, or she is in her primary school classroom. The children are sitting around her in a circle on the classroom floor, listening to 'Miss' telling them a story. They are rapt. One little girl is twiddling with her pigtails and sitting on my mother's lap. Then my mother is upstairs at home, at her sewing machine, the old black Singer, with a dress pattern laid out on the floor and her feet pedalling away at the treadle. That's her, making pastries, making her own clothes, but never ever 'making do'. She was far too proud for that.

All this comforts me. I am not praying exactly, it's more a remembering, my thinks are my thanks, but it could be seen as a form of prayer.

We believe in many things, sir.

If I get through the challenges ahead of me in the coming months – no, *when* I get through the challenges ahead of me – I am going to be more philosophical, with a clearer sense of perspective.

More positive.

Well, that's my intention anyway. If you live defensively, if you play too defensively, never offering a shot, with your bat tucked in behind your pad, simply trying to survive, hoping that the umpire won't spot what you're up to, you may increase your chances of staying out there in the middle, you could be at the wicket for a longer time, going nowhere, *living and partly living*, just occupying the crease, not scoring any runs, not giving any pleasure, but is this what you are in the game for? All you are doing, if you play that way, is slowly digging yourself into a bigger and bigger hole.

If that is what you're doing, if that is all you are doing, are you batting at all, are you really alive? What's the point of just surviving if you never put any runs on the board, if you don't express yourself fully?

The guide and I talk of our children, about their reading habits, their interests, their problems, their characters, the joys and the tensions of bringing them up. His are still at school. He asks me about my children, and how they both became involved in the world of writing. How did Ed become a writer *and* a cricketer? It is a question I am asked every day in India and have never once been asked in England.

His son, our guide says, is mad on cricket, so is his wife. She loves all the Indian cricketers. He smiles. All of them, every cricketer. She is always checking the cricket scores on the internet, always checking the scores, sir, and now his son is doing the same, he himself can never get even to sit at the computer. Is never possible. We laugh at that. His wife's favourite player is V V S Laxman. A good choice, I say, I like the way he stands so still and so tall at the crease and just strikes it.

-All you need is love, he says with a smile.

-It certainly helps, I say.

-No, no. *All* you need is love.

-And a few other things, I say.

-The Beatles, he adds.

The love of children is the most universal of languages; it draws us all together. I do not know enough about the religions or the caste system or the politics of India but we can cross borders and boundaries and become close to each other simply by talking of our children.

As we walk away I pass a young English couple in the street. Their voices are tense. He is having a difficult time with her. She is not happy with him. It's in her walk. 'I know what I said,' the man says to her, 'but I didn't mean it. All right? I just made a mistake.'

She does not answer. She walks on, staring straight ahead.

I would like to tell him I know how he feels but of course I don't.

24

Superstition

Why, having turned away from religion when I was twenty, do I always visit churches, cathedrals, temples and mosques? Why when I am on a walk in any part of London or Kent, in any village or unremarkable town or on holiday in any country, do I 'do a Larkin' and end up alone inside a church and always at a loss much like this? Is it that hunger in me, that *hunger to be more serious*, is that what it is?

Even more, why has superstition become such a problem in my life? Why do I allow myself to be dominated by an absurd portfolio of beliefs, not that they even merit the word beliefs, most of them acted on in the cause of and in the context of cricket? I know it is all craven nonsense. Superstition is unreasonable, it is based on fear and ignorance. If you follow it you enslave yourself to it and you end up dependent on the most groundless rubbish.

I am not just talking about not walking under ladders and being wary of the number 13. Why do I change my shoes or shirt or tie or toothpaste if I think or imagine or misremember (my favourite Hillary Clintonism) that this is what I was wearing/cleaning my teeth with the last time my team or Ed did well. Only mad people carry on like this. And I am not mad. If anything I have often been criticized for being too sane, too reflective, too normal, too balanced, if not a bit lacking in primary colours.

So what on earth do my socks/tie/shirt/shoes/ toothpaste (this is only the merest sample, the list is too embarrassingly long) have to do with anything? By the way, I ought to say straightaway that ties and socks can be a particular bugger, all that changing and fiddling and re-tying and bending and pulling on and then you miss the bus. In the summer months just getting washed and dressed and out of the front door can be more exhausting than a workout. No need for me to join a gym, forget Pilates.

And the cupboard under the bathroom sink is now stacked with every kind of toothpaste; we've got a bigger range of toothpastes to offer guests than we have cereals, and we do have an awful lot of cereals. For a while the old-fashioned Euthymol seemed to be doing the trick, then Aquafresh became my banker, before I lost patience with them both and hot-headedly switched allegiance to Sensodyne (for those with sensitive gums, for those fans who are getting a bit long in the tooth). In one of Ed's spells of low scores, an upsettingly bad run, I was backing all the horses by mixing all three toothpastes on my brush at the same time and fitting those small amounts of all three toothpastes on the bristles took me extra time (and we only have one bathroom, sorry everyone, when it comes to *en suite* we're very off the pace, probably better to book yourself into a hotel), so I locked the door in case anyone caught me doing this, and I have to say I did not like the look on my face in the mirror's ambush. If I was sitting opposite that bloke on the underground I would move my seat.

So because the gods are up there and because we believe in many things, sir, here are some of the standard remarks you absolutely cannot say. Only a madman would utter:

'He's going well.'
'We're going well.'
'It's going well.'
'We do look a good side.'
'He's right on top of his game today.'
'Well, one thing's for sure, we can't lose this one, not even we can lose it from here.'

I have of course in my time said all of those, and after saying the last one I was still stumbling around the ground half an hour after the last wicket fell, still in shock and unable to trust myself to drive home, when I saw coming the other way people in the same state, if not worse, stragglers coming back from the field of battle, shell-shocked, white-faced, wounded, staring, having supped full of horrors. Our faces could have been used in one of his films by Roman Polanski.

And most terrible of all, it was my fault. I should never ever have said: 'Well, one thing's for sure, we can't lose this one, not even we can lose it from here.' It was a salutary, stinging lesson.

Disaster can also strike in the most domestic of contexts. One Sunday Gillie and I could not get to the ground and we were watching Kent's game against Surrey on Ceefax (yes, I do know you can't actually watch a game on Ceefax, you can only follow the panels of scorecards on the screen). On this afternoon Ed was going along nicely, very nicely. Today the gods were smiling down on him, or perhaps they were busy zapping someone else, his name on the screen had not changed from white to blue, he was purring up through the 60s, the 70s and the 80s, finding the boundary easily as he does when he's going well, and his hundred was near, he was in the late 90s, so near and yet so far, and the nervous nineties can get to the fans just as much as to the performer, and suddenly Gillie said:

-Why don't we turn on Radio Kent and hear what they're saying?

-Don't, I said.

-Why not? I'd like to listen for a bit. It's better than staring at a silly Ceefax scorecard.

-Just don't, I said. That's all, just don't.

So she went to find the portable radio. I called after her:

-Please do not do that.

-Why not?

-Because I am begging you not to.

-I'm worried about you, she said as she walked back into the room, tuning in to the familiar voices of Radio Kent Cricket.

107

-Oh, dear, what a delivery! A yorker speared into his leg stump. The perfect yorker. He's yorked him on 99, and that, sadly, is the end of Smith.

I was speechless with anger at her stupidity. Sometimes it is difficult to know what to do with a woman who behaves like that, especially one who should know better, a woman who knows the gods of cricket and their caprice, and even after all these years there was not a hint of repentance or apology.

Another habit I have – and strangely this has been known to work – is always to say good things about the opposition. The thinking here is that by that very act of insincere praise and supposedly even-handed generosity I will both buy my side more runs and get the other side out cheaply. It is the opposite of *schadenfreude*. It is a despicable form of currying favour with the enemy's minders. When I am giving this one an airing I go for:

'Good bowler, this bloke.'
'Always gets a stack against us, this guy could play for England.'
'They're a strong side.'
'We're up against it today.'

Mind you, the benefit to local charities from my superstitions is significant. With the tension building up on the morning of a match, buying my milk and my apples and my newspaper, I often put a bit more than usual into the St John Ambulance box on the counter because well you never know and someone up there in the gods' pre-match studio may be keeping a twenty four hour watch on this shop and may be looking to reward my gift in kind. Once a whole pocketful of coins in the Air Ambulance box brought about a hat trick for Kent at Northampton. Fact.

But the clinching evidence, as so often, concerns how we react to big money.

One summer holidays I was walking down Tonbridge High

Street – I was in my twenties then, this was way back – and I was doing a bit of hurried shopping before dashing off early to see Kent play a big one dayer, a Benson and Hedges quarter final at Canterbury, when I saw in the gutter a brown ten shilling note. A ten shilling note was worth quite a bit then. You want to know how much, do you? Well, I'm not sure exactly how much ten shillings would be worth in today's currency let's think of the equivalent oh it must be about, look I don't know, do I, a few drinks anyway.

Anyway, I knew a ten shilling note was enough to be missed by whoever dropped it. I stooped down and picked it up and dashed off to the police station on the corner of Pembury Road to hand it in. But before I got half way there I stopped, I was just outside Woolworth's in fact, because I realized that by the time I had gone to the police station and added half an hour for the form being filled in by the duty officer who couldn't find a pencil I would more than likely miss the opening overs at the St. Lawrence Ground in Canterbury, which was about an hour and a half's drive away – this was before the M2 and M20.

So, with the extra ten shillings in my guilty back pocket, I drove off in my maroon Mini, lovely sunny day, Kent countryside looking at its best, you just can't beat England when it's like this, can you, why go abroad, who'd want to live anywhere else when there was a loud bang and my windscreen shattered and the tiny bits of glass went all over my trousers and my sandwiches and the front seats and my Buddy Holly tapes and I spent three hours sorting it all out, not to mention coughing up £15 for the replacement windscreen, which meant I missed the whole day's cricket, and of course we lost.

Am I a learner?

A year or two ago, it was early May and bluebell time and the light was filtering between the leaves and I was walking through the woods a few miles from Sir Philip Sidney's

Penshurst Place, when a shaft of sunlight suddenly picked out something purply red just before the sloping blue carpet began. It was about six feet to the right of the path. I stopped and looked more closely and picked up a thickish wodge of £20 notes.

The notes were damp: they must have been lying there a good while. How many hours I wondered had the unfortunate loser spent retracing his steps and scrabbling around in those woods? I looked around. No one in sight.

When I got back to Southborough I tried to find the police station so that I could do the decent thing, only to discover that there was no police station, yes there *had* been a police station in Southborough the butcher said but it had recently relocated, well I should have known it would have, along with the public toilets (sorry these toilets are now closed, so there's no point trying to bash your way in, that's why there are padlocks and bolts everywhere, you'll have to hold on if you can, your nearest public convenience is now in Aberystwyth).

So I went instead into the Hospice In The Weald Charity Shop and handed over the money to a well spoken silver haired lady. It seems obligatory for charity shops to be staffed by well spoken and attentive silver haired ladies who can both speak perfect English and do mental arithmetic. What a combo. What's more, she was the spitting image of my Aunty Eva. She looked down at the notes and then politely but steadily she looked up at me. I told her no I was not being generous and I had not had a nervous breakdown and I had played no part in the fifty million recently stolen at Securitas, Vale Road, Tonbridge, and that, unless she had any objection, I wanted The Hospice in the Weald to put the money to a good use.

Just before I put the key in my front door, as I was taking off my walking boots in the porch, my mobile went. I knew who it was and I had a good feeling.

110

-Hi, it's me.

I could tell by his tone of voice.

He was just out, but he – and his favourite bat – had made 116 against Lancashire.

25

Bats

> This thing here, which looks like a wooden club, is actually
> several pieces of particular wood cunningly put together in
> a certain way so that the whole thing is sprung, like a dance
> floor. It's for hitting cricket balls with. If you get it right, the
> cricket ball will travel 200 yards in four seconds and all you
> have done is give it a knock like taking the top off a bottle of
> stout, and it makes a noise like a trout taking a fly. What
> we're trying to do is write cricket bats. So that when we
> throw up an idea and give it a little knock, it might travel.
>
> Tom Stoppard, *The Real Thing*

Cricket bats can be as sweet as a nut. Cricket bats can be
goers. Or planks. They either pick up well, with a beautiful
balance, or they don't. They may have great middles or they
might have dead areas. Some are all edges. Some flatter to
deceive. Some, though, are wands, like an inspired poet's pen,
his pen is a wand of power, and in the right hands these bats can
seem an extension of your body and soul as you weave your
spell at the crease.

Whatever, you need to put time in on them, to look after
them, they need loving care, that's for sure, because they're an
important part of your life.

Hey, try this one.

Pick this one up.

Feel nice?

Smack.

That is a beauty, an ab-so-lute beauty.

You pick them up, you stand them up, you spin them round
in your hands (like Alec Stewart did), you stroke them, you
grip them, you turn them over, you smell them, handle them,

play with them, reject them or love them and protect them till death or an irreparable split in the wood you do part.

Chuck me a couple, would you?

Smack.

Wow!

Another.

Smack.

Fetch that.

No need to run for that.

Feels good, does it?

I'll make millions with this one.

You have your favourites, some come to mean more to you than others, even when they're beginning to go at the edges and then all but gone you tape them together with loving care, this is one you can't bear to part with, this one brings you luck, it's been with you right through your best run of form, it's a very special bat this one, but even the special ones break, and when they do break they break just like a little girl.

When Bruce Springsteen joined Bob Dylan on stage in 1995 and they sang *Forever Young* together I had tears running down my face. My father cried easily at a Welsh hymn or a Welsh poem or the Welsh team running out at Cardiff or at a favourite view of Pen-y-Fan or there would be a family gathering round a winter's coal fire and I would look across the room and there he was, hanky out, gone.

Thinking of Dad brings back *Goodbye*, a poem by Alun Lewis. The son of a schoolteacher, Alun Lewis was born near Aberdare in the Cynon Valley, in the South Wales coalfields, and was briefly a teacher himself. He died, aged 29, in Burma in 1944. Written for his wife, *Goodbye* is one of the finest of love poems.

As you read it you are, in the least intrusive and most tender way, there with them.

So we must say Goodbye, my darling,
And go, as lovers go, for ever;
Tonight remains, to pack and fix on labels
And make an end of lying down together.

I put a final shilling in the gas,
And watch you slip your dress below your knees
And lie so still I hear your rustling comb
Modulate the autumn in the trees.

And all the countless things I shall remember
Lay mummy-cloths of silence round my head;
I fill the carafe with a drink of water;
You say 'We paid a guinea for this bed,'

And then, 'We'll leave some gas, a little warmth
For the next resident, and these dry flowers,'
And turn your face away, afraid to speak
The big word, that Eternity is ours.

Your kisses close my eyes and yet you stare
As though God struck a child with nameless fears;
Perhaps the water glitters and discloses
Time's chalice and its limpid useless tears.

Everything we renounce except our selves;
Selfishness is the last of all to go;
Our sighs are exhalations of the earth
Our footprints leave a track across the snow.

We make the universe to be our home,
Our nostrils took the wind to be our breath,
Our hearts are massive towers of delight,
We stride across the seven seas of death.

Yet when all's done you'll keep the emerald
I placed upon your finger in the street;
And I will keep the patches that you sewed
On my old battledress tonight, my sweet.

What on earth would my father have been like, sitting in front of his hopeless television screen in Sennybridge, peering through the snowstorm reception as Ed came down the steps at Trent Bridge? That's Ed, Dad, in his England sweater. 'No, is it?' How would he have handled the emotion as his grandson's name was announced over the loudspeakers? He'd have been all over the place.

I have tried hard not to be like that, I reacted against all that, reacted against Dad's overflowing Welshness: I was determined to be suspicious of tears but it's no good, it's in me. Take that Alun Lewis poem, I couldn't read it out loud in front of an audience, I would never get through it, there are some things you can't control, well come to think of it there are quite a few things you can't control, and perhaps you need to be old enough not to care about all that and I am old enough now and I don't care about all that and it feels great.

So, let's take any accusation of sentimentality on the chin. Let me see, before I go to sleep tonight, if I can remember some of Ed's bats from four years old. Can I list them? The stickers changed over the years, and only a lifelong follower would know all this stuff, but some of them were:

- a size 3 SS (signed by Don Bradman)
- a size 5 Magnum VR (signed by Colin Cowdrey)
- a Wisden Special (made from Kashmir willow)
- a Dynadrive size 6 (a plank)
- a Zenith harrow
- a Zenith full size (his first full size)
- a Newbery ('Feel this one go, Dad.')
- a Gunn and Moore (Man of the Match, Under 19 final)

As for the gloves, we won't even go there.

Then, from eighteen onwards, there were professional contracts in the post and annual visits to the factory where his bats were specially made for him. The Slazengers and the Kookaburras started to arrive thick and fast, and if he got a hundred on television he was paid a fee and it was goodbye to his childhood.

26

Acquainted with the night

I have been one acquainted with the night.
I have walked out in rain – and back in rain.
I have outwalked the furthest city light.
I have looked down the saddest city lane.
I have passed by the watchman on his beat
And dropped my eyes, unwilling to explain.
I have stood still and stopped the sound of feet
When far away an interrupted cry
Came over houses from another street,
But not to call me back or say good-by;
And further still at an unearthly height
One luminary clock against the sky
Proclaimed the time was neither wrong nor right.
I have been one acquainted with the night.

Robert Frost (1874-1963)

It was the night after visiting the Taj Mahal, and tired though I was I could not sleep. This is happening to me more and more. Despite all the walking up and down the steps of forts and temples, and despite a few large glasses of The Macallan before our supper, I could not settle. The truth was, I could not get the hospital I am going into – and for some reason its huge car park – out of my mind.

Lying very still in my bed I passed the watchman on my beat and dropped my eyes, unwilling to explain. I did not want to talk to Ed about my fears. Nor did I want to lie awake all night thinking about them. I tried deep breathing (controlled-under-my-breath-deep-breathing so that I would not wake him), but that did not do the trick.

So I switched to some fairly sophisticated counting games.

Counting down from 100 to 0, I imagined I was writing each number in long hand with a piece of chalk on an old-fashioned squeaky blackboard. And I religiously did all this in the belief that it would bore me to sleep, but it only failed to do so in a very boring way.

And then, and I do wish I hadn't, I flicked memory channels and started to tread water, recalling some of the nicknames unfortunate boys were landed with at my school, branded with, boys I played cricket and rugby with, and for a while remembering the nicknames brought a grim smile, then a growing sense of disbelief.

Were they called these names to their faces? Openly? Yes they were. I can hear the names now. There was an Awful and a Horror and a Bugs and a Fairy and a Maniac and a Turd and a Bombhead and a Cough Drop. What would I have felt if I had been called those names? I stood in the shower and I called myself Awful Smith, Horror Smith, Bugs Smith, Fairy Smith, Maniac Smith, Turd Smith, Bombhead Smith and, last but not least, Cough Drop Smith.

By the time I had finished that little march-past of nicknames any remnants of the grim smile on my face had gone. Were they scarred for life?

So I tried to think only happy happy thoughts, but in Agra that night (with the Taj Mahal just across the river) I could not outwalk the light, and even my happy happy thoughts could not get the mad monkey and the huge car park off my back.

At about three o'clock Ed whispered,

-Are you all right?

-I'm fine.

-No, you're not. What is it?

But I managed to deflect him and soon I was over-revving, talking in a random way about the family holidays we had spent in Cornwall and France and Spain, about the mountains we had climbed in Wales and R S Thomas's poem *The Bright Field*, one of the poems I had brought along, the sunlit field that makes up for all the others, and about certain animals that given half a chance I would happily have shot.

It wasn't the poetry or the mountains, it was the last topic – the killing – that really seemed to perk Ed up.

-Which animals would you have shot?

-Those dogs down in St. Maximin for a start.

-The ones that howled all night?

-Yes.

-St. Maximin 1990? That place where I had to sleep on the sofa?

-I'm not sure of the year, I said, but they're the ones. If I'd had a gun with a silencer, if I could have got away with it, I'd have crept out of bed and leant out of the bedroom window and lined them up and... bang.

-No you wouldn't.

-And the ones in Northern Cyprus, you weren't with us, Mum and I were staying outside Kyrenia, in Bellapais, near the abbey, that's Lawrence Durrell country, *Bitter Lemons* and all that, Lawrence was the brother of Gerald, Gerald Durrell, *My Family and Other Animals*, set in Corfu, you must know about the Durrells, no? no, of course you've never heard of either of them, ignorant sod, anyway those Cypriot dogs were even worse than the French ones, well they were more like wolves than dogs, they threw themselves head first like front row forwards at the corrugated iron fencing, and they kept the racket up all night, *all night*, they were hunting dogs, they were caged in and deliberately starved so that they were up and raring for the kill on Thursdays when they were let out for their weekly hunt. And when they weren't headbutting the corrugated iron they were whining and drooling and barking.

-You can't hear drooling, Dad.

-They were that close to our bedroom window.

-It's not their fault they were caged in.

-No, I'm sorry, it was behaviour beyond any kind of exculpation.

-You must try to keep calm, didn't the doctor tell you that?

-I'd have shot them, Ed.

-No, you wouldn't.

-Without a qualm.

-No you wouldn't, you have qualms about everything.

-And the squirrels, I'd shoot them.

-Are we in France or in Cyprus now?

-Kent. They've taken over Kent.

-Bit of an exaggeration, isn't it?

-No, they've taken over our garden. Fact. When there were just a few of them, when they were few and far between, I thought they were quite sweet nipping around the place in their bright bushy-tailed way. Good God, how wrong can you be! They do not know it yet, they may think they are setting the agenda, they may think they are *numero uno* in our garden, but the days of the Kentish grey squirrel in our neck of the woods are numbered.

-Dead squirrels aside, Dad, where do you put the Taj Mahal? *Numero uno*?

-We're talking Wonders of the World?

-We are. Is it above or below the Alhambra?

We had been to Andalucia in 1995 – to Malaga, Seville, Cordoba, Ronda and finally Granada – and in Granada we went, as go you must, to visit the Alhambra and the Generalife. We walked around the arcades and past the myrtle hedges, the pavilions and the oriental gardens, the patios and the running water and the light and the aromas, and I thought this is it, these boys got pleasure right, this is a pearl of great price.

The Alhambra was the nearest I have yet felt to heaven on earth, though walking early one spring morning round Rydal Water in the Lake District, the lanes laced with frost, walking where Wordsworth walked man and boy, ran it close.

I heard Ed roll over in his bed.

-Anyway, he said, back to sleep. It's all right for you but I've got to be up in a couple of hours.

119

He had arranged an early morning call to take some photographs of the Taj Mahal at the crack of dawn. And when I next woke up he (and the hospital car park) had gone.

27

The Tables Turned

Up! Up! my friend, and quit your books;
Or surely you'll grow double:
Up! Up! my friend, and clear your looks;
Why all this toil and trouble?

The sun, above the mountain's head,
A freshening lustre mellow
Through all the long fields has spread,
His first sweet evening yellow.

Books! 'tis a dull and endless strife:
Come, hear the woodland linnet,
How sweet the music! On my life,
There's more of wisdom in it.

And hark! How blithe the throstle sings!
He, too, is no mean preacher:
Come forth into the life of things,
Let Nature be your Teacher.

She has a world of ready wealth,
Our minds and hearts to bless –
Spontaneous wisdom breathed by health,
Truth breathed by cheerfulness.

One impulse from a vernal wood
May teach you more of man,
Of moral evil and of good,
Than all the sages can.

Sweet is the lore which Nature brings;
Our meddling intellect
Mis-shapes the beauteous forms of things:-
We murder to dissect.

Enough of Science and of Art;
Close up those barren leaves;
Come forth, and bring with you a heart
That watches and receives.

William Wordsworth (1770-1850)

28

Walking

I am a walker, though nowhere in the Wordsworth or Edward Thomas league, and I am certainly not one of those *serious* walkers you see in increasing numbers these days on the hills and coastal paths of England. That is, I do not move forward with those special metal things, those hiking sticks or Nordic poles, which look as if you would be better employed piercing litter in a public park or tidying the verge of a motorway. Nor do I have a plastic covered Ordnance Survey map hanging round my neck. No, as my wife points out, I am above all that: I just get lost.

But, following Wordsworth, I do like to get away for a while from the strife of books, from all that reading and writing and analyzing: I need to give myself a break from my meddling intellect and my tendency to murderous dissection.

Walking not only clears your looks, it clears your vision and, if you're up for it, it makes you listen. Walking makes you attend. It sharpens your inward ear. It is all the more baffling, then, when you are out in beautiful country to come across so many walkers with their iPods or headphones on – zombies with their eyes glazed and their attention locked into a recorded world. Why not go the whole hog and put on a blindfold?

For a writer with tired eyes and a headstorm there's nothing better than putting down your pencil and stepping out *into the life of things*, getting out and about in the lanes, over the fields, up the hills, the views getting better as you gain height, accepting what Wordsworth calls *the ready wealth* of Nature.

Mind you, I also like drifting down into the valleys and sloping along the canal towpaths, especially if there's a bottle of wine as a homecoming. Most days I might be out there at any time, on my own, semi-aimlessly, vacant for a few hours. You've probably seen me around. You might even have been a bit worried on my behalf.

If nothing else walking gives me, as I've said, an enforced rest from the toil and trouble of too much self. Sometimes I might be mulling something over, something I am writing, but then again I might just as easily be physically wide awake but rather empty-headed.

Or I might be bored. Boredom – feeling flat and dull, feeling overtaken by lassitude – can be a necessary part of the creative cycle, or at least a pre-condition. If you're not bored by yourself, when you should be, you can end up thinking that your perceptions of the obvious are brilliant insights.

Whichever way, when I am walking I like to take my time. It doesn't matter if it is cold or hot, wet or dry. It can be all weathers. Not that I am what you might call a power walker. There are dynamic-aerobic-calorie-burning women who power past me at a rate of knots, toning their bums, thighs, hips, shoulders and abs. They wear me out. They make me want to sit on a stile or lie on my back in the middle of a field, looking up at 'the magpie veering about, a magpie like a weathercock in doubt'.

And it doesn't have to be in one of those wild places to which Robert Macfarlane transports us. Nice if it is, of course – what better than the crags and cataracts of the Lake District, or watching a gap open up in the clouds above Snowdon, or, closer to home, stopping for a breather on a sun-warmed boulder in the Brecon Beacons? – but it needn't be a scene so dramatic. It doesn't have to include Coleridge's thundershowers and waterfalls and precipices. If there's nothing else on offer, I'll just pad along suburban streets and communal parks and slip unseen in and out of towns.

When I walk I suppose I am thinking about something, there must be something going on up there, but if so it is of the most inconsequential kind, random and unstructured and all over the place. I'm not sure a real thinker would even rate it as thought. But then my intellectual journeys, like my walks, have never followed any route. I have never had an intellectual map. I find what I find, I stumble around, trying to come to terms with whatever lands on me. I walk and I write because I have to walk and I have to write and while I am doing so stuff sometimes happens.

But then again all too often stuff all seems to happen.

Perhaps walking enables me to take a break from solipsism, to tug myself free from my discontented self, and even if it does not give me a break, it offers me a larger home. I usually leave my house when I am troubled or weighed down or taut or because I sense I am fooling myself over something, or when I have cold feet about a paragraph and the right words are refusing to choose me. And wordlessness, as I know to my cost, can all too easily lead to a sense of worthlessness.

Some days I set off when I am indecisive or a victim of whispering mood swings, when my self criticism is running rampant and my self-belief paper-thin, or when I am unable to see my way through some cloudy matter, perhaps something that is niggling me in my family or in a friendship, and by the time I am back home and pulling my shoes off outside the back door – without even consciously confronting the problem – as often as not the weight has lifted, it has often sorted itself out.

Solvitur ambulando
It is solved by walking.

Have I naturalised myself?

As well as being a balm to a troubled soul, as well as putting a distance between you and your pencil or your computer, walking can paradoxically also write sentences for you: it can unblock the path ahead. Pastoral solitude and silence can wake you up, can kick start you. All journeys, and I can't remember who said this – I used to have this quotation in my diary but I now can't even find the diary – all journeys have a secret destination of which the traveller is unaware.

****

In cricket, by the way – and we're going well off piste here – in cricket saying 'I am a walker' means something quite different. It has nothing to do with the landscape or clambering over stiles. It means that as a batsman (if you have nicked a catch to the wicketkeeper) you do not wait for the umpire to give you out. You simply deliver the verdict on yourself. As a matter of honour and honesty you very decently decide to give yourself out. You become both the judge and the jury on yourself. As a batsman you metaphorically hold up your gloved hand and say yes, lads, I did indeed hit that, yes the faintest of touches, but hit it I did and I am out and I am setting off back to the pavilion without the umpire even needing to raise his finger.

This kind of conduct, this particular form of walking, is very controversial. On both sides of the walking debate cricketers get very worked up. If you even mention 'walking' to some cricketers things can get nasty because it opens up the question of who stands on the moral high ground. In a game still much concerned with codes of conduct, is walking the right way to behave? Is it the case that the heroes of the past always walked?

Far from proving you to be decent and honest and saintly some cricketers see walking as a dodgy assumption of superiority. The walker can appear self satisfied and smug. After all, is it up to the batsman to decide these things? Why should the batsman be his own judge and jury? That, the non-walkers contend, is the umpire's job. That is why the umpire is standing there, poor chap, in his white coat. The batsman is not – and should not be – the master of his own fate.

And anyway do walkers always walk? Is the walker a man to be trusted? Walking can be a grey, murky issue plagued by subtle forms of dishonesty.

Some walkers I have known walk very happily when they have a decent score but do not leave the crease quite so promptly at other times. They are what you might call selective walkers. If they have batted beautifully and have, say, 120 on the board and unexpectedly nick it they're jolly decent and off they go to the pavilion before the finger of fate goes up, but if they are on 0 or scratching around on 3 and they get the faintest of touches they look what-me-guv innocent and get the benefit of the doubt from the umpires because they are known to be walkers.

****

What on earth would the walking non-cricketing poet Edward Thomas, sitting there quietly in the corner of the pub smoking his pipe, have made of all this? I don't know. He may not have had a clue what we cricketers at the bar were talking about, but even if he had never held a bat in his hands I think he would have enjoyed the scrupulosity of these distinctions.

Of course by any standards Edward Thomas, like Wordsworth before him, was a proper walker. These guys didn't go for a stroll or a constitutional. Edward Thomas and his friend, the American poet Robert Frost, not only 'outwalked the furthest city light', they covered many a Gloucestershire mile together. But Thomas – a tall figure, with a slight stoop and piercing eyes – was usually out there on his own, striding along the chalky tracks and bridleways of Wiltshire with an edition of Wordsworth in a specially made pocket. I sometimes carry a small edition of Edward Thomas in mine, an easy thing because he only wrote one hundred and forty four poems.

Thomas walked partly to make a living from the prose books that came from his cross country tramps, though the income proved more a pittance than a living. And, it has to be said, many of these prose testaments, with titles such as *Light and Twilight* and *Horae Solitariae*, may smell appealingly of wood smoke but they are not very good. His deeper need, it seems to me, deeper even than the need for money to sustain his wife and children, was to walk away his melancholy, to ward off his pessimism. 'I am not at all sure that I am on a wise path – far less a profitable one.'

Gone, gone again,
May, June, July,
And August gone,
Again gone by,
Not memorable
Save that I saw them go,
And past the empty quays
The rivers flow.

On these walks – mentally sketching – Edward Thomas watched ploughmen and shepherds at work or passed a word with a stranger in a lane. He liked solitary swimming. Some days he spoke to no one, not a soul, until he stopped at a pub for a meal and a bed. He didn't talk unless he had something to say. He was a listener who hated labels.

Sometimes by chance, though sometimes because I am drawn to do so, I have walked many of the same roads as Edward Thomas and in many of the same places. Not only in mid Wales, but in the Weald of Kent where I live, and around Petersfield and Sheet and Steep in Hampshire, near Bedales School, in the country of Gilbert White and Cobbett. And in July 1977, without discussing it much, Gillie and I felt it right that we should name our son after him.

As well as walking in his footsteps I have for the last thirty years or so followed Edward Thomas as a writer. It was not that I sought him out or danced attendance on him, more that he crept up on me and fell in step with me and became my guide. My hero. And it's not only me. For a whole community of writers he is a model: the way that he watches and absorbs, the way he attends to the commonplace, the way he doesn't

Go Big, and, most subtle of all, his instinctive avoidance of any insidious neatness.

He has been my litmus test on subject matter ('anything, however small, may make a poem; concentration, intensity of mood, is the one necessary condition') but most especially in his insistence that language should not be betrayed.

Because if anything has been betrayed in recent years, and far too much has, above all it is language. Spin, by definition, is language betrayed, as in what the spin doctors call the 'creative presentation of facts'. That is a debasement of the word 'creative' and a debasement of the word 'facts'. The only master of spin I would pay to watch is Shane Warne.

****

I am not a poet but if I could have written just one good poem in my life I would like it to have been *As The Team's Head-Brass*. It is set in England during the First World War just before Edward Thomas (then in his late 30s) enlists for action. In this poem – appropriately enough he is on a walk – he charts, as he tends to do, an everyday experience and pinpoints an everyday moment. Like his most famous poem, *Adlestrop*, it is anecdotal. He has stopped at the side of a field and sits on a fallen tree, as any of us might do, to watch a ploughman at work. The poet and the ploughman soon fall into intermittent conversation about the weather, then about the war. (Change the plough and the team of horses to a tractor and it is the kind of scene you can still see and enjoy many a day in England.)

In a natural and unforced way, with no spin in sight, Edward Thomas has caught here just about everything that matters. He has touched on all the big issues, the watermarks of experience, and yet there is no striving after any of them. He touches on life, death, nature, time, love, loss, the random nature of fate, our need for human connection, and the off-hand, not to mention the almost whimsical manner in which the English choose to speak about cataclysmic events. That is how we talk. That is how, at our best, we use language.

And Edward Thomas achieves all this without seeming to do so. As an apparently inconsequential work of art it strikes me as maddeningly good.

With the lightest of brushstrokes, so light you could miss realizing that Thomas has done it, the lovers frame the poem. Thomas's eye spots the couple going into the wood and later catches them coming out. Whatever terrible mess we may make of this world, and however little we seem to learn from our past mistakes, there will always be lovers.

And the poem ends with images of the horses stumbling and the clods toppling, images that subliminally move us from the corner of this quiet English field to France and to Flanders, a crumbling and a stumbling and a toppling that reflects and in retrospect prefigures the death of the poet. Edward Thomas was killed by a stray shell at 7.36 one morning while at his observation post. He is buried at Agny, just south of Arras, in a small military cemetery down a lane called La Route Verte. I have been to see his grave.

Second Lieutenant
P E Thomas
Royal Garrison Artillery
9th April 1917

Am I sounding like a teacher?

I am.

But as I am, I might as well add that I have encountered a misunderstanding, which may muddle an important moment in the poem. The first question 'When will they take it away?' is spoken by the poet not by the ploughman.

29

As the Team's Head-Brass

As the team's head-brass flashed out on the turn
The lovers disappeared into the wood.
I sat among the boughs of the fallen elm
That strewed the angle of the fallow, and
Watched the plough narrowing a yellow square
Of charlock. Every time the horses turned
Instead of treading me down, the ploughman leaned
Upon the handles to say or ask a word,
About the weather, next about the war.
Scraping the share he faced the wood,
And screwed along the furrow till the brass flashed once
more.
The blizzard felled the elm whose crest
I sat in, by a woodpecker's round hole,
The ploughman said. 'When will they take it away?'
'When the war's over.' So the talk began-
One minute and an interval of ten,
A minute more and the same interval.
'Have you been out?' 'No.' 'And don't want to, perhaps?'
'If I could only come back again, I should.
I could spare an arm. I shouldn't want to lose
A leg. If I should lose my head, why, so,
I should want nothing more... Have many gone
From here?' 'Yes.' 'Many lost?' 'Yes, a good few.
Only two teams work on the farm this year.
One of my mates is dead. The second day
In France they killed him. It was back in March,
The very night of the blizzard too. Now if
He had stayed here we should have moved the tree.'
'And I should not have sat here. Everything

Would have been different. For it would have been
Another world.' 'Ay, and a better, though
If we could see all all might seem good.' Then
The lovers came out of the wood again:
The horses started and for the last time
I watched the clods crumble and topple over
After the ploughshare and the stumbling team.

Edward Thomas (1878-1917)

30

Pessimism

When it came to which cricket club I should play for once I left school there was no choice. I joined The Pessimists. The Pessimists played all over suburban Bristol and the surrounding area, though sometimes we set out, full of foreboding, for rural Somerset or Gloucestershire. We were a travelling club – that is, we had no ground of our own – so we contributed the match ball each Saturday and we paid for the opposition's teas as well as our own. And while there were many clubs I might have considered, such as The Optimists, I had no doubts.

It may be a geographical thing or just fate, I don't know, but when it comes to the dead sea of pessimism most Bristolians are out and out naturals. And for those of us with a sceptical cast of mind cricket is the best game in the world. It tends to pessimism. It is irreconcileable with hope. It savours more of pain than pleasure. Failure is written into the grain of the bat. The willow is weeping. And each Saturday afternoon the accuracy of your gloomy predictions and the wisdom of your philosophy was revealed and reinforced.

At school and at university, as I have already indicated, I had read all the Greek tragedies. They did not go in for happy endings. Man is born unto trouble as the sparks fly upwards. I know, I'm a bowler. Nor had I ignored the French dramatists: I had read my Racine and my Corneille. Closer to home, I had read my Marlowe and my Webster. And the first book I published was an edition of *King Lear*, and some of the most memorably simple lines in that play ring all kinds of cricketing bells:

'Howl, howl, howl.' (This one's for bowlers.)
'Never, never, never, never, never.' (For aggrieved batsmen.)

Then there were the novelists and the philosophers. I had read *The Mayor of Casterbridge* and *Tess of the D'Urbervilles* and *Jude The Obscure*. And, as if all that was not enough, I had even dipped into Schopenhauer and Hartmann and remained sane.

So I felt very much a part of The Pessimists from my first game – especially as I was run out and had a catch dropped at slip off my bowling – and when I was back with my family on vacation from Cambridge or at home on holiday from Edinburgh (where I started my teaching career) I always wanted to join up with them. I identified with the side and liked every one of the players, starting with the captain, John Jolly, the most perfect name for any captain of a club called The Pessimists, and sometimes I was laughing so much as I walked back to my bowling mark that I could not start my run up.

If you asked a fellow Pessimist fielder how things were going when you passed him between overs he would never say: 'Really well, we've got them on the run.' He would say: 'Early days. Remember last year, it could still go tits up from here.' In much the same way I knew I would be a friend of my doctor when I was sitting in his surgery and he described life as a losing rearguard action: that, I said to myself as I picked up my prescription, is a man speaking after my own heart. For Christmas I gave him Philip Larkin's *Whitsun Weddings* and we never looked back.

The moaning and lamenting in the pub after a Pessimists game was epic in its scope. It was also sensationally detailed and comprehensive. Over beer or scrumpy it usually started with the wicket keeper complaining about – and showing us – the bruises on his hands from trying to catch our throw-ins and the fact that no one bothered to back up and that meant overthrows and it kicked on and deteriorated from there: gutless batting, no application, wayward bowling, bowlers bowling at the wrong ends, bowlers bowling too short or too full, slips standing too deep, crap umpiring, shit wicket, and if this is how it's going to be (and on this every Pessimist player in the pub was agreed) what's the point in going on when we could all be spending the afternoon shopping with our wives and girlfriends.

-So, see you next Saturday then, Gren. Well batted.

-Yeah, cheers, Sam.

-Look after yourself. Well bowled, son.

-Nice catch, Steve.

-Thanks. Pick you up next Saturday just after twelve at the roundabout, right?

There was one more significant factor which made this club feel like home from home. My brother David played for them (later he was the captain, and a very good one) and after our childhood years one-on-one in the school playground there was every reason for me to be on the same side.

In fact in the summer of 1963 David and I had one of our happiest days together. My Tripos results at Cambridge had come through. I had my degree and I vowed I would never take another exam.

Never, never, never, never, never.

At the very same time David had passed his accountancy finals. That Saturday we played for The Pessimists at Winscombe in Somerset and to put the icing on the cake I got a very rare 50. True, I missed the first three deliveries, any one of which might have bowled me, but I hit the rest smack in the middle of the bat.

Easy game, cricket.

Afterwards we sat on the grass under a spreading chestnut tree drinking and watching the sun go down – it was all very Thomas Hardy and all the better for that – so, that's a beer for me, please, and a cider for David, and then another beer for me and another cider for David. One more? Why not? And why not two more? But didn't Michael Henchard sell his wife when he was pissed? Never mind, silly to move on when everything feels so right. Don't get 50 every day of the week, do I? Well, don't get one every decade either. As the Somerset daylight left us and the night wore on I replayed and rewrote my 50: I was now *rifling* a few fours past extra, and hitting their bowlers to all corners of the ground, pie-throwers all of them. In my complacent idiocy I was now playing shots all round the wicket, cuts, smack, pulls, smack, easing into Tom Graveney drives, and our adult lives seemed to open out before us, and all was promise.

31

A good day for a pessimist

That was how things were (on a good day) when I was eighteen or twenty-one or whatever, and the cricket scene was a bit like that for me during the following ten years or so. For Ed it was very different. At eighteen he was picked for the opening match of the 1996 first class season. It was his first class debut, Cambridge University v Glamorgan. It was played at Fenners, on the ground where I had spent all those happy hours as a spectator in the early 1960s.

As an undergraduate I was always worried about my work. I worried, full stop. Even so, worried or not worried, after a couple of lectures in the English Faculty I would cycle up to Fenners, cutting across Parkers Piece, and I would be sitting there on a wooden seat on my own. Since arriving at St John's in 1960 I had new heroes, the Light Blues in rugby and the Light Blues in cricket. But I was always sitting there at Fenners with a book. Well, I was revising, wasn't I, probably re-reading *Oedipus Rex*, no, it was more likely to be a critical book, more than likely it would be *The Harvest of Tragedy* by T R Henn, and I would be watching Brearley and Craig open the batting for Cambridge, and very good they both were. Both were philosophers as well, not a bad thing to be, a philosopher, if you hope to remain mentally intact as an opening batter.

Ed was down to open against Glamorgan, batting at number one. He was a freshman. Before the side was picked for the Glamorgan match we were not sure that he would be playing though he had been in the side for the pre-season one dayers against Loughborough and Durham Universities. But there his name was in the papers. He was still only eighteen.

What was my day like?

Well, as usual I spent it teaching, it's what I do, and that afternoon (I've checked in my workbook) I was looking at some sections of *A Shropshire Lad* by A E Housman, poetry steeped in death, yes, it's what I do. After school I did some umpiring, before finishing up with a play rehearsal. While I was teaching, and even more when I was umpiring, I found myself mentally filming the day's play at Fenners, and being me it turned out to be a horror film. I could see Ed at the crease. Bits of action flickered and replayed before me. He had nicked out for 0. Green wicket, overcast morning, he plays forward with hard hands, it seams away, he nicks it, regulation catch behind. Pity. Did he play the line or did he follow it? Slow walk back. Can happen to anyone.

Or the ball nips back, keeps a bit low, smack in front, stone dead, finger up, LBW. Pity. Should he have played forward, should he have got a bigger stride in?

Easy to criticize from the boundary, easy from the armchair.

Early season is always difficult.

Oh, well.

He gloves it down the leg side. Keeper takes it. What a death.

They bowl it full and wide, asking to be driven and he drives, it goes wider, thickish edge, second slip takes a great catch. I told him not to chase the wide ones. I did tell him to leave those wide ones well alone, didn't I?

Glamorgan, as so often in the past, had a good seam attack led by Steve Watkin, and then there was Robert Croft with his crafty off spin.

Would Ed be out of his depth? Dads don't like to see their sons out of their depth. Was this the day that he was found out?

Stop it!

I had to stop. This could go on for years. Stop it now.

These were not coping strategies. I was driving myself mad. I could feel myself raising my umpire's finger against my own son.

Fortunately the challenge and the excitement of a play rehearsal always puts everything else on the back burner. You can't multi-task, thank God, even women can't when you're directing a play. When you're directing *Death of a Salesman* on stage you forget the drama of the cricket field. Thank God for Arthur Miller, for another world, a world much bigger than mine.

When I got home he rang.

-Hi. It's me.

-Hi, Ed.

I always like to hear his voice after a game, whatever has happened on the pitch, and I can usually tell by those three words, by the tone of that opening, what kind of day it has been.

-Seen the scores, Dad?

-No, just got in.

He had made a hundred. Then Becky rang. She had never doubted him. There is a hop, skip and jump in her voice. I told you, *I told you*, she shouted. Gillie got in from work. She had never doubted him either. Well, I stand guilty. I played for The Pessimists and I had doubted him.

Unless you're a Bradman, unless you're a 'ledge', there can be long spells in cricket when things don't go well, when you wonder not only where the next hundred is coming from but where the hell the next run is coming from, wondering whether to adjust your technique or to change your mental approach, or should you just trust in yourself and believe in all you have learnt over the years, and hope for things to start going your way?

And when they do go your way, when we get a bit of success in sport, we tend to keep the celebrations in our family. Then brother David rang. He not only has an extraordinary grasp of the game's history and statistics, but has published a number of books including one about the early years of first class cricket in Wales. No other cricketer, he said, had ever scored a debut hundred against Glamorgan. He also thought – but he would have to check this – that Ed was not only the youngest person ever to score a hundred on debut for Cambridge but also the youngest undergraduate to make a hundred there at any time.

Really?

What about Brearley?

What about Craig?

Didn't Brearley?

Didn't Craig?

Names hurtle past.

Going back earlier, what about Peter May?

Ted Dexter?

No, David said. Hubert Doggart scored a double hundred on debut but he was 22.

I felt giddy.

Even in the world of sport, where today's rooster is tomorrow's feather duster, this was a day. Whatever the future brought Ed, whatever ups and downs lay waiting for him on the road ahead, this was a day.

That evening I went down to The Castle pub on the River Medway at Tonbridge. At the bar there was Paul Taylor, the master in charge of the Ist XI, and then Chris Stone, the Tonbridge School coach, came in. Both had done so much for Ed, as Chris Stone was later to do for Kent. We shook hands and drank deep. I had a lot to be thankful for. I stood there in a daze. The beer tasted so good. I wasn't even sure where I was or whether it had really happened. (No, it had happened. I had checked Ceefax. Then checked it again and left it on.) We all grinned and nodded and raised our glasses and I sat down on a bar stool only to stand up again and as I bought another round I understood the cliché: 'It doesn't get much better than this.'

Talk about optimism.

32

To An Athlete Dying Young

The time you won your town the race
We chaired you through the market-place;
Man and boy stood cheering by,
And home we brought you shoulder-high.
Today, the road all runners come,
Shoulder-high we bring you home,
And set you at your threshold down,
Townsman of a stiller town.
Smart lad, to slip betimes away
From fields where glory does not stay
And early though the laurel grows
It withers quicker than the rose.
Eyes the shady night has shut
Cannot see the record cut,
And silence sounds no worse than cheers
After earth has stopped the ears:
Now you will not swell the rout
Of lads that wore their honours out,
Runners whom renown outran
And the name died before the man.
So set, before its echoes fade,
The fleet foot on the sill of shade,
And hold to the low lintel up
The still-defended challenge-cup.
And round that early-laurelled head
Will flock to gaze the strengthless dead,
And find unwithered on its curls
The garland briefer than a girl's.

A E Housman (1859-1936)

33

A Passage to India

I taught at the same school for many years. That is – in my profession's obligatory and defensive phrase – I taught there *for more years than I care to remember*.

Sorry.

And one of the first things I ever heard about Tonbridge School, before I had even unpacked my bags and taught my first lesson, was that the novelist E M Forster had been very unhappy there as a boy. Now, I have no wish to be either dismissive or defensive about Forster's time at Tonbridge but here is what he actually wrote about Sawston, the school in his novel *The Longest Journey*:

> Sawston owes something to my own public school. I was neither very happy nor very unhappy there. The best of my life began when I left school, and I am always puzzled when other elderly men reminisce over their respective public schools so excitedly and compare them as if they were works of art: it sounds as if they must have had a dullish time since.

As a matter of interest could I ask you how were your own schooldays? Were they the happiest days of your life? Or deeply miserable? Or were they 'neither very happy nor very unhappy'? And what about all those boys and girls I see every rush hour morning in their school buses? Are those boys and girls happy/unhappy in normal measures?

Anyway, would it be so odd if E M Forster was unhappy at school? Susceptible, creative people are eight to ten times more likely to suffer from depression and mental illness. In her book *The Midnight Disease*, the neurosurgeon Alice Flaherty makes this clear: amongst artists, painters, actors, writers, philosophers and musicians the levels of anxiety and depression are disturbingly high, massively higher than amongst politicians, business people or scientists.

Sometimes, too, may there not be a tendency to over-dramatise one's schooldays? If it is a commonplace, as it is, for older men in club ties to lie repeatedly about their sporting achievements at school, may it not also be common for the more creative spirits retrospectively to point up their unhappiness? To make the most artistic use of their adolescent victimhood?

I have no wish to glamorize teenage melancholia. Perhaps, though, it is the sense of exclusion, of not quite fitting in to a family or community, of standing at an angle, that sense of being off the pitch, which sharpens the critical and creative faculty.

As a teacher I did what I could do when I sensed unhappiness, believing that the best pastoral care at my disposal was trying to come up with a good lesson, trying to amuse or stretch or lift especially those pupils I felt might be feeling low, to imply by a look or an off-hand remark that I was on their side, rather than sitting them down for a long talk and telling them that I felt their pain. I was a teacher and try as I might I was not a therapist with a one-to-one appointment book.

And a confession now: when I was a schoolboy in Wales, I tended to embrace my boredom and to hug my unhappiness, if unhappiness is what it was. So, was it all a bit of a game? I'm not sure, sometimes yes sometimes no, but for me being pissed off was probably my first professional role. And then, as you know, I happily threw my lot in with The Pessimists.

It seems, then, that the years from 13 to 18 are unlikely to be easy, unless you fit like a hand in glove with your school, and those that do rarely achieve much in later life. There's a lot of unresolved anger in teenage, and a lot of unresolved tension in creative people. They – or is it we? – they/we can have therapy

I suppose, and in some cases that may well help, but there is at the very least the risk that if you delete the doom and gloom, if you take away the demons, you take away the angels too.

I have kept a diary for only one full year of my life, and if that diary is to be believed – the reliability of diaries being a moot point – things weren't a barrel of laughs for me in 1956.

Mind you, I was fourteen. And bored.

Most mornings in Brecon, it would seem, started with a breakfast of shrapnel (my word for bacon) and fried bread. Then chapel. After chapel there was double Greek, *ie* double Xenophon, with a group of Welsh boys trying to translate the dreary Greek historian (born *circa* BC 430) into English. That took me to break, when you will find me joining the long queue winding its way into the tuck-shop for a hot doughnut. After break there was double Latin, *ie* double Livy, with the same group of Welsh boys trying to translate the slightly less dreary Roman historian (born BC 59?) into English. Lunch was leather (translated as liver) and onions. After lunch, as you know by now, I was out on the playing fields hitting a ball or kicking a ball or being kicked.

Next day, *semper idem*, not much different.

For Forster, as for me, life really began when he went up to Cambridge. There he was happy, there he found his spiritual home, and at 25 he was on the edge of a period of astonishing creativity. Here are his New Year Resolutions:

One.   Get up earlier.
Two.   Smoke in public. It gives a reason for you, and you can observe unchallenged.
Three.   Plan out work.
Four.   More exercise, to keep the brutes quiet.
Five.   Don't ever shrink from self analysis, but don't keep on at it too long.
Six.   Get a less superficial idea of women.
Seven.   Don't be so afraid of going into strange places

or company.

Eight. Be a fool more frequently.

By the time he was in his late 20s, aided by a modicum of boredom and necessary routine, he had already written three extraordinary novels, *Where Angels Fear To Tread* (1905), *The Longest Journey* (1907), and *A Room with A View* (1908).

In January 1913 – with *Howard's End* (1911) also under his belt – he was in India, visiting Jaipur and Jodhpur, and a bit more at ease with his homosexuality.

****

The other main thing I heard about Tonbridge before I got there was that Colin Cowdrey had played for the Ist XI at Lord's when he was only 13. Cricket and cricketers would without a doubt have been the very last thing on Forster's mind – he felt rejected by the sporty types – but I can't help making the connection because in 1932 Colin Cowdrey was born in India, and I have come to know almost as much about Colin Cowdrey's cricket as I do about the novels of E M Forster.

I wonder what they would have made of each other had they met: EMF and MCC, the non-cricketer and the cricketer, often both known by their initials. They were both so English. In their differing ways they were both sensitive and shy and defensive men. They were both gentle but steely, complex and driven. But they both knew, beneath their subtle natures and their modest exteriors, that they were special. With a pen or a bat in hand they were geniuses.

In 1913 E M Forster found the cities of Jaipur and Jodhpur 'pink and purple and golden with the desert beyond'. Much more important than the colours in the landscape Forster also found there, as he found wherever he went in India, 'a sense of immense freedom, not even a long sea voyage could prepare you for it'. Jaipur and Jodhpur offered him an escape from the tentative worlds of Tunbridge Wells and Weybridge.

In his own private, liberal way Forster would 'have the time of his life'. He would not, at long last, have to worry too much about 'lapses'. Indeed, far from being a sin which led to punishment, a lapse in India would not even be a lapse. It would be a natural pleasure.

Going to India, for Forster, would be a kind of 'Hindu holiday'. Carefree but exploratory, he travelled by train or by elephant or jammed tight inside a tikka gharry. He noted that the English language is, for an Indian, a subtly different tongue with different idioms and different tones. He found good-looking young men with beautiful skins, he found 'fine, fierce youths' and charming boys with animated voices, as well as a vast country which gave him the inspiration for his greatest novel, *A Passage To India*.

In his diary and in his letters he was soon noting:

> 'Nothing will hurry Elephant, and she is so huge that she has to take a great circuit round each corner.'
> 'Both sorts of camel.'
> 'Got into the electric tram ... road blocked by buffaloes and goats and sweetmeat sellers and pariah dogs.'
> 'Donkeys with hens and babies tied to their backs and sometimes quarrelling.'
> 'Costumes not brilliant, but a sense of splendour through dirt.'
> 'They talked louder and louder as Indians do when they are happy.'

Pink and purple and golden Jaipur with the desert beyond, and that is the desert Ed and I will cross. Pink is the colour of hospitality and the pink in Jaipur is far more than a superficial wash on the city walls. The whole place, founded by the astronomer king Sawai Jai Singh, feels friendly. Our hotel, the Samode Haveli – in its heyday a palace – is right in the heart of the walled city, only yards from the swirling streets, yet it does not seem so. Royal residence it may have been but it is private and courteous and intimate and warm.

There is also live music. Or put it another way: there is no naff hotel soundtrack. From the first evening, with dinner in the courtyard under a full moon, accompanied by musicians and followed by a puppet show, I felt I would like it here. And sitting by the pool in the morning, surrounded by red bougainvilleas and acacia trees, I could see black kites soaring and twisting high above me (though in fact they are brown raptors with shallow forked tails) as well as the red and blue paper ones. For this is also the time of the annual paper kite festival.

While I am staring up at the sky a member of the hotel staff brings me a couple of faxes. One is about the film we are planning to make from one of my novels; the other is from my oldest friend from Cambridge days, now living in Athens, giving me the details of surgeon he has heard is good. As I put the faxes away I notice that the man who brought them is still hovering.

-Mr Smith, may I ask you a question?

-Yes of course, please do.

-Is it true that Mr Edward is a cricketer?

-Yes, he is.

-Ah, I wanted to be very sure. They rang from the hotel in Agra to say that he was a cricketer but you know, sir, with some people in Agra you never know. Is he, would he be, the Smith who played for England?

-Well, he's one of them. But there are many more famous cricketing Smiths. There's Mike Smith and Robin Smith, and plenty of others. We're pretty thick on the ground, we Smiths.

-On which ground is it that you Smiths are thick?

-No, I meant there are a lot of us in England. A lot of Smiths. We're everywhere, that's all I meant.

-And do you think Mr Edward would talk to us about cricket? There are many of us here who have asked me to ask you.

-I'm sure he would. He'd love to.
-Thank you. I will bring your tea.
-Thank you.
-With milk cold.

34

A father at Lord's

In 1995 (thirty five years after my season as captain at school) Ed was in his last year at Tonbridge, and the standard of cricket in Kent was much higher than in my own Welsh schooldays. There was much more talent, the pitches favoured batsmen, the coaches were better, and the fixtures much tougher.

Not that I saw much of Ed batting in 1994 and 1995 because I was always in the nets or umpiring on some far distant field, but colleagues sometimes told me about this or that innings of his, and how he had struck it, and when I got home in the evening we would talk at length in the garden or up in his room and I would find myself asking him all the usual questions:

'How did you play?'
'How did you get off the mark?'
'Defence solid?'
'Were you fencing outside off stump?'
'Leg side OK?'
'Rotating the strike?'
'How did you play the spinners?'
'Were you hooking the quicks?'
'Did you slice it through the gully?'
'How did you run between wickets?'
'How did you get out?'

And occasionally I took my life in my hands and risked the most irritating question any father can ask his son, the Mike Agassi question, the question that changes the atmosphere, which is, given that you were well set and going strongly, and given that you had done the difficult bit and were into the twenties, *should* you have got out?

In other words:

Did you play a crap shot?

Because if you go on playing crap shots like those when you're well set you won't go very far in the game, will you, Andre?

Will you?

However many shots like those he may have played, however often he fenced or sliced and got himself out, Ed still left school with a Ist XI average of 70+, an average that has never been bettered, which is not to be sneezed at, and early one June morning the following summer Gillie and I were driving up to North London for the Oxford v Cambridge match.

It was his first game at Lord's.

This wasn't as big an event as that packed ground for the Kent v Middlesex Nat West Final in 1984. As a day in the cricketing calendar the Varsity Match was quite a few notches below that in sporting significance, and it is dropping lower each year, but emotionally it was a notch or two up on the family Richter scale, if there are notches on the Richter. It was twelve years since that big cup final, and far from being a full house there would only be a sprinkling of spectators for the Varsity Match, but this was our son who was out there.

Tom Graveney I had idealized and identified with from a distance; Chris Cowdrey I knew well and cared about; but following your own flesh and blood is something else. Flesh and blood, as any heart-in-his-or-her-mouth parent knows, makes all the difference. This time Ed would not be a fan with us in the Mound Stand, he was no longer that little boy sitting next to his sister and tucking early into the sandwiches, but a young man up on the players' balcony and, more to the point, soon to be out there in the middle.

And a blue.

When I was an undergraduate, back in the early 60s, how glamorous it seemed to be a blue. Blues were gods. They walked around the college in a light blue scarf and a light blue sweater and a light blue aura. As they passed you on the way to lectures or cycling to the sports fields your eyes registered 'blue'. Even a lacrosse half blue had a very slight glow.

By June 1996, and still only eighteen, Ed had a couple of first class hundreds under his belt – the debut one I've mentioned against Glamorgan and then a second one against Sussex at Hove. He had briefly been top of the first class batting averages, and what's more, I had photographed the page on Ceefax to prove it. There had been a lot of press interest in him, much of it premature, with headlines worryingly regular. The media makes you; the media unmakes you. All that attention, as I knew too well, guaranteed absolutely nothing. Pump up their tyres too much, pump up their tyres too soon, as John Inverarity puts it, and they are more likely to burst. Very little guarantees anything in cricket.

Anything can happen on the day.

Russell Cake, the Cambridge captain, and Ed opened the batting. As Ed walked down the pavilion steps in his white helmet and took guard we were watching in a swirling confusion of pride and anxiety. He made 40 and 50 in that Varsity Match, and he hit a few sweetly, and I know he hit a few sweetly because this time I had my eyes only half closed. Not much of an achievement maybe in the great scheme of things, half closed eyes, but still a small step in the right direction.

I was further cheered that day at Lord's by the mother of one of the Cambridge players telling me that she always went straight to the lavatory the moment her son went in to bat. You won't understand this, she said to me, I can see you're one of those blokes who takes it all in his stride. It's just a game to you, you men, she said to me, but I simply can't stand it, I hate every minute of it, I can't bear to see my little boy upset, it is such a cruel game, cricket, it's the worst of all games and I wish he'd never started playing it, it just makes me miserable.

I smiled and played along with the idea that I was one of those blokes, one of those blokes who could take it on the chin.

Men, eh?

I wonder how long she stayed in the Ladies that afternoon. Did she lock the door and sit down and pray for her son? Or did she stand up on the seat and listen at the window for any tell-tale sounds of his fate on the field? But how on earth, stuck in there, would she find out how he got on, how long he was in, and how many (if any) he had made? How would she know when it was time to step down and return to the Long Room?

Did her husband go in and bang on the door and say it's all right you can come out now, love, it's all over, he's LBW, shocking decision?

If I ever meet her again I'll ask her.

35

R E Jones, poet

To tie up the Cambridge connection and to end the thread of my schooldays in Wales, I want to return for just a moment to R E Jones. In *The Learning Game* I wrote about the influence of Bob Jones on me. This is how I saw him:

> He taught literature with a religious rigour. Indeed he taught it as if his life depended on it. English literature, not classics, was the central discipline to him. His eyes burned. His classroom felt more like chapel than chapel. He had been a pupil, which means a disciple, of F. R. Leavis at Downing College, Cambridge, and he brought some of that personal edge and partisanship to his lessons. I didn't quite know what was going on but something was and I liked the smell of uncompromising contempt: always heady stuff for an unresolved boy. It meant you could put your boot in.

I did not add that as well as directing me in *A Winter's Tale* – I played the part of a minor lord, Cleomenes, and I am annoyed to find that it is one of the few things I still know off by heart – Bob Jones coached the Ist XI in cricket. Though short in stature, Bob bowled quickly and aggressively in the nets, with a good glare, and he was not at all averse to roughing you up. As with a lot of fast bowlers I have faced he quite liked hitting you.

Some years later Bob had moved on from Brecon to a new post in Coventry, whereas I was now up at Cambridge and going to some of Leavis's lectures myself.

One weekend I jumped on a train for Coventry. Partly I wanted to see the new cathedral because my uncle and aunt had been in the city on the night of 14th November 1940 when wave after wave of the Luftwaffe flew over. That night they killed over 500 people and destroyed over 4000 homes, as well as most of the old cathedral. In the new cathedral I wanted to see the controversial Graham Sutherland tapestry and the John Piper stained glass Baptistery windows.

But deep down I really wanted to see Bob Jones.

After standing in front of the Sutherland tapestry (my father had told me it was dull) and the Piper windows (my father had told me they were magnificent, and he was bang on with both assessments), I took a bus out through the Coventry suburbs and in the course of that evening I found out, for the first time, that Bob was a poet.

How strange it is, when you are young, to discover that your teachers have another life beyond the classroom, to realize that they are actually alive somewhere else, and that they may even know women and girls.

So it was a strange moment when Bob left the sitting room – I won't call it an epiphany because I'm sick and tired of every piddling thing being called an epiphany, as if every first experience is a Second Coming – but it was a strange moment when he went into his study, and returned with some loose sheets of paper. He said he had so far only shown these poems to his wife.

I held the pages in my hand. There were three or four poems, poorly typed. What a private thrill. But what on earth was I going to say to him? He was the teacher, not me. Yes, I was reading English at university and at the same university he attended but this was different, this was personal. It was one thing being clever-dick dismissive about some dead novelist or putting down some American literary critic but quite another if the poet was alive and lighting a cigarette and sitting right there opposite you, waiting.

Was I expected to pass some kind of judgement or simply to approve? I didn't know, and I certainly cannot now recall what I did say. Knowing me a bit, as I do, I probably did a lot of mmm-ing.

Mmm.

Yes.

Yes.

Mmm.

I like it.

In truth, I haven't a clue what I did or said but I hope I got away with it. But as I read his poems, and privately noted the influence of W H Auden, I do know I felt very special. I felt I was being treated as if I was grown up, as if I knew something, as if, at long last, my opinion counted.

Heady stuff.

Things were looking up.

Once again those two threads, literature and cricket, were weaving together in my life or at least running on parallel lines: searching for the right word, getting into the swing of things, practising hard, striving for the right line, not over-hitting it, trying to turn a phrase, developing a greater range but not getting ahead of yourself, learning to be patient, learning not to force the pace, and coming to terms with the frustrations of form.

Bob Jones died of cancer, aged 50, in 1976.

Here is one of the poems I held in my hand, many years back, that evening in an English teacher's house in Coventry. It has, I have to say, stayed with me more vividly than the Sutherland tapestry or even the Piper stained glass windows. And given all that has happened to us both since, re-reading it feels a bit like facing one of Bob's fast short balls in the nets, as it rears up and hits me just below the heart.

36

Years back...

Years back I used to chuck them down quite fast.
Place end to end the wasted hours I spent
With fingers cradling seams, trying to move
A shiny globe away towards the slips,
Or whip one back from off to leg, inside
Fatally hurried forward defensive shots:
The crazy column stretches to the moon,
Appropriate for all those lunacies.
And even now there is a kind of urge
To sway the body fully from the hips,
Even, when unobserved, to turn the arm.
Insidiously, the thing's been getting worse.
A kind of stifled tensing of the muscles
Surprises me in sedentary tasks;
Lying in bed at night, I catch myself
Accelerating smoothly to the crease,
Perfectly balanced in delivery strides,
Following through, and scattering the stumps
More comprehensively than in the past.
The more I get my youth into perspective,
The more this young man peers down sunny wickets,
And bowls his way out of this slackening frame.

R E Jones (1926-1976)

37

Three in the morning courage

There is a vulture high above the Fort, a white-rumped vulture, and no sooner had I spotted it than Ed started to talk to me very openly about what is coming up when I get back to England. No, 'what is coming up when I get back to England' is the sort of euphemism I am determined not to use. Speak plainly, Jonathan, or not at all.

Speak what we feel, not what we ought to say.

A line from the last speech in *King Lear*.
I agree.
Dead right.
Start again.
With the vulture circling above, Ed started talking to me about my surgery. The date is fixed. He encouraged me to consider it as a part of the car that needs sorting out, no more and no less. It was important that I accepted that something had broken down, something was not functioning in my body and had to be fixed. Don't take it personally, Dad, he said, don't see it as your whole body, and certainly not as your whole self. You, he said, remain you.

As far as my body went, that was fine. But what about my mind?

When the mind's free, the body's delicate

In the middle of the night how do you get the mad monkey off your back? Where is my three o'clock in the morning courage? Three o'clock in the morning courage, Napoleon Bonaparte reckoned, was the rarest courage of all, and I would agree. Move it on an hour, to four in the morning, and Larkin is trying to face down his fears:

Waking at four to soundless dark

How do you shut up the jabbering voices in your head, the voices you do not want to hear? I am finding it difficult. I am finding it difficult, if not impossible, to stop my mind racing ahead to depressing scenarios. 'The locusts are small but many and they eat up every green thing in the land.' Striking a brave attitude is one thing, and we can all say something upbeat to friends on the telephone; but maintaining your determination in the middle of the night is another.

Being brave lets no one off the grave.
So...
Courage.
Bon cou-rage, mon ami.
There's no other way.

From this strongly fortified position in Jaipur, looking down on the gardens and the reflections in the lake, and looking down on a long line of elephants (smaller than the African elephants), all that Ed said makes sense. Can I manage that objective view of my condition? Being objective has not always been my strong suit but I will try. If I can I will try to see it that way, as a bit of gardening. I shall say to myself that the surgeon is doing a bit of pruning. That's all, just a bit of pruning. And if it comes down to metaphors I do prefer pruning trees to the MOT, I do prefer the garden to the garage. Chekhov, a leading observer of life and a potential captain of my Overseas All Stars XI, loved gardening.

'Mass suicide happened here thrice,' our guide Vorcha says, pointing to a spot in the Amber Fort, and her sentence has regained my attention.

She tells us in some detail about the mass female suicides, but rather than a floorful of bloody corpses it is her wonderfully old-fashioned use of the word 'thrice' that sticks with me. I have never heard anyone say the word 'thrice' before. Written, yes, of course, I've seen the witches' lines from *Macbeth* written and I have heard the lines read aloud often enough in my classroom:

Thrice to thine, and thrice to mine,
And thrice again, to make up nine

Come to think of it, there are plenty of thrices in *Macbeth*:

Thrice the brinded cat hath mewed
Thrice and once the hedge-pig whined.

And of course I know the word from *St. Mark's Gospel*:

Before the cock crow twice thou shalt deny me thrice. And when he thought thereon he wept.

But I had not heard it spoken so naturally in modern English. Not for the first time in India, charmed by the unfamiliarly familiar, I find myself smiling in admiration. (Further on and deeper into the palace, as we were peering into the Maharajah's dimly lit bedroom, Vorcha said, 'I can read writing on wall. Can you?' It took me a beat to work out she was speaking literally. We peered hard until we could.)

And if I say 'thrice' to myself now not only does it trigger the lotus flowers and the marble screens and the Maharajah's bedroom, but a surgeon's knife and my first white-rumped vulture.

38

Is he going to make it?

One of the many joys of teaching is sensing you have spotted someone of extraordinary potential. When Vikram Seth was in my class it never struck me that he might become the author who would write *A Suitable Boy*, a great novel, but I did think he might well become a great man. And if I had been pressed to put my money on which field he would shine in I might have said economics or politics.

Can you tell when a young sportsman or a young musician or a young actor is 'going to make it'? Can you sit in the classroom or in the stand or in the auditorium and watch the broad river of talent flow past and follow your instinct and back your hunch and say: *'That's* the one to watch. That boy will go all the way?'

Sometimes you can, sometimes you can't. Some are dead certs. Some flatter to deceive. Some look as if they might train on. It's a very exciting moment when you are sure enough of your judgement to back someone all the way...

In 1997 we decided to produce the Scottish play. At the school I taught at there were plays performed every month of every term, all kinds of plays for all age groups, perhaps ten or fifteen plays a year, but I had always shied away from *Macbeth*. When it came to decision time on that play, as with Marlowe's *Dr Faustus*, I somehow always lost my nerve.

This time we grasped the nettle.

'We' were Lawrence Thornbury, a professional actor who teaches drama, and me. We loved working together and auditioned for a couple of weeks, with a large number of seventeen and eighteen year old boys coming along, some of them very gifted.

At the auditions we moved the parts around, as you do,

switching from one boy to another, Macbeth, Duncan, Banquo, Macduff, Malcolm, Ross *et al*, trying to give all those who turned up a chance to impress while masking our own casting instincts. We had a long list of names to choose from, almost an embarrassment of riches. There were bound to be many disappointed people.

One afternoon a boy in his first year in the school, aged fourteen, turned up and asked if he could audition. We said of course you can, thanks for coming along, very good of you, great, but you do realize, don't you, that we usually tend to cast the more senior boys in this one because... well, because it's the most senior play, isn't it, it's the big one, and it may be their last chance while they're at school, you'd feel the same if you were a senior wouldn't you, fair's fair *etc*. And which part did he want to read for? There were, after all, a couple of parts for younger boys.

Let's see...

Well, there is Fleance, the son of Banquo.

Nice little cameo, as long as you can run.

And there's Lady Macduff's son.

Nice little cameo, precocious, nasty death, think *Sopranos*.

One of those might be up for grabs.

Not big parts but they're pretty dramatic moments.

No, he said, if it was all right with us he wanted to read for the part of Macbeth, but if he didn't get it he'd be happy to try for Macduff or – since we brought them up – Fleance or Lady Macduff's son, or be given any role. But first he would like a shot at Macbeth.

Macbeth?

Yes.

Right.

After he had read a few lines – well, he didn't have to read the lines because he had obviously learnt large swathes of the play – I felt my hands and neck and back go funny:

Be innocent of the knowledge, dearest chuck,
Till thou applaud the deed. Come, seeling night,
Scarf up the tender eye of pitiful day,
And with thy bloody and invisible hand
Cancel and tear to pieces that great bond
Which keeps me pale. Light thickens, and the crow
Makes wing to the rooky wood.
Good things of day begin to droop and drowse,
Whiles night's black agents to their preys do rouse.
Thou marvel'st at my words; but hold thee still,
Things bad begun make strong themselves by ill.
So prithee go with me.

I put my pen down. We had a problem. This young boy was already much better than many of the professional actors I had worked with at the BBC. His voice, a voice to die for, his range, his focus and his intelligence, they all hit me. Lawrence and I looked at each other, eyes widening but trying to hide our responses.

The other boys and girls stood still. Whatever this boy's age, they all knew that they were watching someone extraordinary.

So prithee go with me.

We were going with him all right, prithee, and so were they. Though no doubt it hurt, they could see the writing on the wall. A few minutes later Lawrence slipped me a folded note: 'I think we might be following his career with interest.'

We cast Dan Stevens as Macbeth, and everyone in the production, even the most disappointed of his rivals, knew it was the right decision. In his following years at school Dan played many more roles, in house plays, in GCSE plays, and in his year group. Lawrence and I directed him twice more: as Thomas Becket in T S Eliot's *Murder in the Cathedral*, which was performed in the school chapel, and in his last year he played Prince Hal in *Henry IV Part One*, the first big production in the newly opened E M Forster theatre.

So in all we directed him thrice.

And, as predicted and as promised, we followed his career. We went up to the ADC at Cambridge to watch him, and – as fate would have it – his first major role there as a freshman was Macbeth. Rebecca Hall was Lady Macbeth. We went to see him in *Hay Fever* at the Haymarket Theatre in the West End when he played with Judi Dench, then we pressed the record button when he was Nick Guest for three weeks, the lead in *A Line of Beauty* on BBC2.

Then came *Downton Abbey*.

39

Heads and captains

As I was in the classroom for forty odd years I must have talked an awful lot. Teachers talk an awful lot to each other as well. Teachers have opinions. And what, do you imagine, was the thing we teachers talked most about over those forty odd years? What did our chats at lunch or on the phone or in the pub or in the corridors (or even, heaven help us, during in the holidays) usually centre on?

Well, run your mind over it, you've been to school and you may be a parent: the possibilities are endless.

Class sizes, the National Curriculum, teachers' pay, the madness of over-testing, our own careers, the facilities for the arts or for sports or for science, dumbing down, the workload, the corruption called coursework, how to release creativity, the top heavy bureaucracy, drugs, the state of the nation's education, the debate between state schools and the independent sector, the ghastly jargon, the league tables.

No, none of those. It was the Head. Simple as that. It was the Head's personality, the Head's character or lack of, and the way he or she did or, more often did not, do things. It was about the leader, the boss. And, massively, it was about his or her weaknesses. (I don't think I can keep up this he/she thing, so I'm settling for he.)

He, the Head, was the problem all right. Well, no, going back a move or two, it was the governors' fault or the fault of the committee who had appointed him in the first place. They'd done their exhaustive consultations and they'd followed their process to the letter and they had come up – as any process followed to the letter tends to do – with the wrong answer. They'd been taken in by the boss's interview performance and by his presentation. Everyone but everyone who had ever worked with him in his previous jobs said he wasn't cut out to be a Head, that the man did not understand human beings, and so it had proved.

But did anyone listen to those warning voices?

Still, too late now, we're stuck with him.

So, what was it about the Head's character and performance?

Well, he either over-worked in his bunker or he went home before midnight, the lazy bugger. He was autocratic or couldn't make a decision to save his life, inflexible or all things to all men, heavy fisted or wibbly wobbly, anal or liberal, puritanical or indulgent, he either listens to no-one or to everyone or to the wrong people, he'd had an unhappy childhood or was smug Middle England through and through, he was either as thick as two short planks or an arrogant intellectual snob, he was a bully or he wouldn't say boo to a goose, he lacked the common touch or had no *gravitas*, he was too aloof or too matey, he was either a self-promoting and already over-promoted careerist or a man who didn't have the first clue about the way the modern world let alone this community worked.

Oh, and staff morale was plummeting.

And one more thing, his wife was Lady Macbeth.

The most civilized dinner parties were, of course, comfortably the worst. Someone would start, in the most understated of ways, to dribble a few drops of poison over the first glass of white wine and someone else would pour it more freely into the red and by the early hours there would be a dead body and a wake and a scattering of his ashes to the four winds. And, I admit, I've joined in with the best of them.

Since I have retired from full-time teaching this scene has been replayed all over the country. In recent years I have visited nearly a hundred schools of all kinds, seeing what they are up to, trying to keep up to speed, teaching a bit here, joining in with classes and departmental meetings there, doing whatever I'm asked. And I have found it is much the same wherever I go. It's the Head's fault.

The other night, getting a bit weary of it all, I took my life in my hands and asked over the soup if we could possibly not talk about the Head, if we could possibly not bang on about whatever latest shocker he had just committed.

There was a bit of a pause. Quite a long pause in fact.

I had spoken out of turn.

I had gone beyond a guest's brief.

The evening was ruined.

Eventually, with his eyes down, the man sitting opposite me protested that they did not do that: I was obviously new to this community, they were very supportive of the management, it wasn't that kind of school at all, and they certainly weren't that sort of Common Room.

Then the table fell into a long sullen silence.

Who'd be a Head? Or, come to that, a cricket captain?

40

Talent and a bit of steel

One thing that was deepening all through the 1970s and 80s, as you'll have picked up from the Nat West Final chapter, was our love of Kent cricket. No, our passion for Kent cricket. During those years Chris Cowdrey and Richard Ellison and Graham Cowdrey – players I had known as schoolboys – were regulars in the county side, and my allegiance to Graveney's Gloucestershire, through my long residence in the south-east, was transferring to Cowdrey's Kent.

It wasn't a quick thing, this transference. It was slow and natural. I had been away from the West Country since my youth, and my life with the Pessimists was now a long time ago, so I did not feel a turncoat, the change felt right, and after all my children were Kent born and Kent bred.

And, anyway, it wasn't Cowdrey's Kent. Nor was it all about boys I had known at Tonbridge School or wherever you were from. The Kent we followed was everyone's Kent and that's what we loved about it: Alan Knott, Derek Underwood, Chris Tavare, Chris Penn, Mark Benson, Neil Taylor, Alan Igglesden, Steve Marsh, Trevor Ward, Carl Hooper, Matthew Fleming and many others meant just as much, as did the team photos, the little flags, the key-rings, the score cards, the Kent annuals, the players' individual photos from the club shop, the autographs: all the obsessively regular features of fandom.

The Smiths were regular, devoted, ordinary, obsessive fans. Some players are special to you, of course they are, you attach yourself to them, drawn to the particular way they express themselves and play the game, but whoever they were, if they pulled on the Kent shirt we were for them till the last ball was bowled.

And all the way home.

Then there were the grounds: the St Lawrence Ground at Canterbury, the Mote at Maidstone, the Nevill at Tunbridge Wells, all atmospheric and beautiful and different, as well as Dartford and Folkestone before they dropped away as venues. I have watched cricket from every angle at all those grounds, from all kinds of seats, in every kind of mood, from inside or outside my car, sometimes glancing down to read a poem or an article or even a short story, but usually with my heart in mouth and my heart on my sleeve for Kent.

I knew everything about the teams, every year, every detail and every statistic, and that included the 2nd XI stats. At work I kept checking the scores by telephoning Kent Cricket Call, often running out in the five minute break between lessons. It was thrilling. It was purgatory.

If I could get away to see any of the games I jumped on a train or into the car. On Sundays we as a family were off on the road, and that included driving to any away grounds we could make, to the Oval, Chelmsford, Northampton, Hove, Guildford, Southampton, Southend, Basingstoke, even as far as Bristol and Worcester, with the children sometimes asleep in the back – what a relief, no more questions – on the way home.

I hated it when fans criticized any Kent players. Sometimes we moved our seats because I found personal abuse very hard to take. It was always me who wanted to move. In particular I hated hearing some fat drunk in front of me (with the top of his sweaty bottom, have I said this before, sadly the image keeps coming round and round on the loop, with the top of his sweaty bottom showing above his saggy jeans) and the same fat man is shouting 'tosser' and 'wanker' at a fielder for dropping a high swirling catch or spilling a fast snick in the slips. Yes, I know that's peanuts compared with the visceral hatred screamed every second of every minute at a football match. I've been to plenty of football matches, but that's part of the point: you don't go to cricket matches to get football, although increasingly you do.

Once we had moved our seats and had settled to a different view I was usually told by my family that I was being over-sensitive. I was told we should have stayed right where we were in the thick of it and taken it on the chin. Becky was always up for returning enemy fire with interest. She does a good glare, she's not afraid of hostility and she does not back down. On a few occasions Ed – aged seven, eight, ten or whatever – would turn on an overheated fan and ask him a few specific questions about the player he was screaming at and cite a few facts. He didn't back down either. They don't back down, my children. Where it comes from I don't know. Me, I've always been one for a quiet life.

In the tea intervals of Kent matches the four of us played on the outfield. The ground was full of fathers and sons (and quite a few wives and daughters) and every kind of ball was in use, tennis balls, rubber balls, 'no cricket balls on the outfield please' over the loudspeaker, you fielded for everyone else and kept a wary eye open in the cross fire because you could be hit by a tracer bullet from any angle. Becky bowled and batted as well, and caught better than any of us. She swooped. She would still be in any slip cordon of mine. Second slip I think.

Quite a few of the young boys playing on the outfield looked as if they might well be good when they grew up. In the twenty minute tea interval on that boundary's edge you could see the promise, the raw talent, the languid movers, the natural timers, a hook off the nose here, a crisp cut there, someone leaning into a drive, a nice high left arm action, an easily taken low catch, those who could bowl a yorker, those with a bit of steel in their narrowing eyes, those who were up for it, those with an appetite.

Which of these young boys all around me might make it in the first class game? Who would blossom? Even as a teacher and a schoolboy coach I did not know.

Talent and a bit of steel and you're getting close, but even that combination will not guarantee that you come through and keep coming through and go all the way. There are many talented, tough-minded players who cannot perform at a high level. Nor can you always tell in the nets. You never really know until they're out there in the middle, with the screws tightening and with the fielders' endless chirping and with the pressure building, day in day out, in all weathers, on all pitches, facing a good and varied attack.

-Here come the umpires.
-Two more, Dad.
-Better get back to our seats.
-Think we'll do it?
-We'll see.
-Can I have an ice cream, Dad?
-No.
-You've got your beer.
-What's that got to do with it?
-Can I have an ice cream?

Right, clear the outfield please. And please cover your windscreens on the bank. The glare gets in the players' eyes.

****

Given all the above, given all those years of being a Kent fan, followed by seven years following him as a Kent player, it felt like a divorce when Ed moved to Middlesex in 2004. It is difficult enough, at the best of times, to be detached or balanced about your team, let alone being detached or balanced about your own children – indeed it is impossible, as a lifetime of listening to parents has taught me – so how much more so when your son leaves the club to which you are emotionally tied. If transferring my allegiance from Gloucestershire to Kent felt slow and natural, moving from Kent to Middlesex was a wrench.

As for when Kent played Middlesex…

Still, life goes on, Jonathan, *live with it*, that's what one of my friends often says to me when I am finding it difficult adjusting to something. He makes it sound so simple, don't make a meal of it, just punch in the new code, that's all, it's easy, and open the new door. Perhaps other people really do feel like that about their lives.

Instead of the St Lawrence Ground at Canterbury or the Mote at Maidstone I was now to be found superstitiously wandering around Lord's, a much grander spot but knowing no-one, and still looking for the special seat that would deliver the goods – a significant score for Ed and a win for his new county. And I also had to decide which advertising board to focus on as the bowler ran in to bowl to Ed. Vital to get that sorted. There had to be coherence to my off-field game.

Was it best to sit in the Allen Stand, or, if I had my jacket and tie, on one or other level of the pavilion? Should I enjoy the sun on the open seats of the Compton and Edrich, or climb up the Warner Stand? On the other hand, if I settled for the front row of the Mound, and Middlesex were in the field, I might catch Ed's eye. He has a way of acknowledging he's seen me, a wave so slight you have to be sharp to catch it.

And as for the out-grounds, instead of knowing every inch of the back roads to Maidstone or Tunbridge Wells, I was sitting in a suburban lay-by, with the Greater London map open on my knees, wondering where the hell I was, is it the A10 or the A11 for Southgate, which exit is it from the M25, or shall we try the North Circular, or, tell you what, why not open the car window, that bloke over there looks friendly, excuse me, sorry to bother you but I'm trying to find my way to Uxbridge.

41

Sensitivity

You can be too sensitive to make it in sport. There is no doubt about that, and cricket above all games ruthlessly exposes not just the quality of your technique and the depth of your talent but also your nerve ends and your psyche. This is nothing to do with being macho.

-All right.

-That's not what you want to talk about, is it?

-All right, no.

To put it at its bleakest, why do so many cricketers commit suicide? Is it linked to the notion that the game makes you die a bit every day? I think it is. Does cricket, more than any other sport, *do your head in*? I think it does. Is it that the severity of the psychological pressure is for some people simply too repetitive and too extended and too remorseless? That it can become unendurable?

The cricket sky can certainly be a cruel blue. It takes you to breaking point. It plays very hard on you, undermining you, turning the knife in you very slowly, stretching you to the limit, testing you, kicking you in the teeth, jumping up and biting you, and sometimes wearing you close to despair. Until one day you crack and you sit with your head in your hands and you find yourself saying:

'Right, that's it, I'm giving up.'

'Stuff this for a lark, it's driving me nuts.'

'I'm crap, I've gone.'

'I'm missing straight balls, I'm retiring.'

Giving up the game is one thing but giving up your *life* because you can't stand it any more? No, as I look at the young boys with bright eyes on the boundary's edge, no, please, no.

You need, then, to be able to take it, to have a certain steadfastness, to be able to hang in there, to have the capacity to endure, to be resilient, to be tough enough to take the rough stuff and to see it through. But as well as taking it on the chin you also need to care and to feel it all, though not to the point that it blows you away or emasculates you.

The point is, you must somehow or other put your sensitivity on hold because you have chosen the arena of public competition. It is a balancing act. You must not be insensitive but you can, I would argue, be too sensitive to make it as a sportsman – and, while we are at it, too sensitive to be a good teacher or a good writer. I sometimes fear, for what it's worth, that I might have been disabled and diminished by my own form of over-sensitivity.

For many years I struggled with this tough/tender dilemma, this anomaly, but then I came across *Sensitivity*, a short poem by Elizabeth Jennings. I found myself nodding at her every word and perception. Says it all, as they say.

Elizabeth Jennings, if you want to know, is always in my Writers XI. 'The sky is a cruel blue' (see above) is one of her lines. I hope it caught your eye and you thought it was good. She writes about nature, about growing up, about struggling to believe in God, and she is uncanny at catching the half-seen and the just-heard.

Decades ago at school, at pre-game pick-ups on some distant football or hockey field, the teacher used to select two captains from the group and tell them to stand in front of all the players and to pick their own sides. It is a pretty simple and ruthless operation. You have first pick, I have second pick, now your pick, now mine, and so on until everyone is on one side or the other and of course it is an absolutely great experience if you are over-weight and have a cold and hate sport and are the last person left unpicked.

Well, at the pre-match pick, in which of course I am one of the two captains, I always surprise the opposition by pointing

at Elizabeth Jennings and saying,
  -You, I'll have you.
  -Me?
  -Yes, you, Elizabeth.
  -But I don't want to play. I'm cold.
  -I've just picked you, you're playing.
  -I hate games.
  -Games are good for you.
  -All the people I hate like games.
  -But you like me, don't you?
  -Only occasionally.
  -I'll look after you. Who knows, there might be a poem in it.
  -I want to sit on the grass and meditate.
  -Shut up, Elizabeth, and get over here.
  -Why can't I meditate?
  -Look, life is tough. Put down your carrier bag and get a red
shirt on, Elizabeth, or I'll put you in goal.

****

I pinned up the team sheet in the games porch:

Jonathan Smith's Indian Tour XI
In batting order

R S Thomas
Vikram Seth
Arthur Hugh Clough
Alun Lewis
Robert Frost
William Wordsworth
Edward Thomas
A E Housman
William Shakespeare
Elizabeth Jennings
Vernon Scannell

12th woman: George Eliot
Scorer: Rudyard Kipling
Meet at pavilion, 1.45 sharp
Clean your boots

Let's admit straight away the unfairness of any team that I select, as well as the obvious Anglo-Welsh bias, and also concede that once you're on my list it is very hard to come off it. Don't worry, you won't be dropped by me in a hurry. I am nothing if not consistent. To be unavailable for selection you have to do something quite appalling like saying that all sportsmen are thick or the only music worth listening to is classical music and the saxophone isn't really an instrument and Andy Irvine of Scotland was a better fullback than J P R Williams of Wales, but short of errors of that magnitude if you're on my team sheet I tend to forgive you just about anything. Once you are chosen I can explain away any of your errors of judgement and justify in sympathetic terms any of your human failings and even defend any bad books or poems you may have written.

****

I heard Elizabeth Jennings read some of her poems at the Cheltenham Literary Festival in 1992. She signed her collection *Times and Seasons* for me. As she was reading *Sensitivity* I was torn between thinking how wonderful this writer is and thinking oh no, it's not fair, not *another* person who's better than I am.

You can be too sensitive
To be an artist at all;
So sensitive that the fall
Of tears comes on in a way
That has no power.
You need to be tough

To feel the rough
Sway of the sea
Yet still be
Swayed by stars, easily
Moved. It is an anomaly.

Great men have had
The needed balance.
Sometimes gay, sometimes sad,
Sometimes, perhaps by chance,
They have been able to enhance
The whole world or indeed
Make a new one:
Plant the seed
Fulfil our need
Blaze out a sun.

Elizabeth Jennings (1926-2001)

42

A cow jam

We're on the road from Udaipur to Jodhpur, *and the road was dazed with heat*, that's a line from a poem but I can't remember which, and we're in the back seats with our bottled water and our bananas and with quite a few near misses already under our belts. At this rate I could well be dead before my date with the surgeon. It's a white knuckle ride. Coming straight at us on the wrong side of the road there is a steady stream of lorries blowing their horns and waving us out of the way while our imperturbable driver is talking over his shoulder about his national team.

They are very good cricketers, the Indians, he said. I agree that they are very good cricketers. Yes, he said, they are all very, very good. What a batting line-up, I say to him, it must be as good as any top order in the world, and please keep your eyes on the road. Oh yes, he says,

-Sehwag, very good batsman. Virender Sehwag.

-Yes, he is, I reply. He smashes it ball one.

-Dravid, very good batsman. Rahul Dravid.

-Absolutely the tops, and such a technique.

-Tendulkar. Very fine player. Sachin Tendulkar.

-None better. The little master. Hints of Bradman.

-Laxman, very good player. V V S Laxman.

-He's very elegant. A bit like Tom Graveney.

-Yuvraj Singh is a very good player.

-He strikes it beautifully, lovely high back lift.

-Ganguly a very fine player. Sourav Ganguly.

-He is indeed, the ex-king.

He seemed, for the moment, to be satisfied with that roll call of Indian batsmen, satisfied with my responses, satisfied with each and every one of his stylish heroes and what a batting line-up indeed, what a talented team, and he said they would surely beat Pakistan in the series about to start the very next day and what a series that would be and then they would surely beat England in the series that followed the series against Pakistan and what a series it would be against England and on he drove, dodging the lorries on the wrong side of the road and the potholes on both sides of the road and anticipating Indian first innings totals of 600 or more against England, indeed why stop at 600, Indians love to make 700, and on he drove happily shaking his head to himself.

-And then there are the Indian bowlers, I said.

Ed elbowed me in the ribs. He had run out of patience. We had just been through all the Indian batters, one by one, and here I was giving our imperturbable driver a further chance to pay his tribute, one by one, to all the Indian bowlers:

-Oh, yes. Kumble, very good bowler. Anil Kumble.

And on we bumped and rumbled, another eye-opening day in India, but all the Indian days were vividly merging into one India, with my memory overflowing: semi-arid land giving way to the fertile, the bright eyed children, the rock hard ground, huge red sandstone forts, the small pigs and the tall camels, swooping parrots, women in bright saris with panniers of earth on their heads, donkeys, tea boiling, vultures, families living by the side of the road, dogs asleep in the sun, until – as often happens in India – we had to stop. You have to stop an awful lot in India.

Usually our driver slowly and skilfully circumnavigated whatever lay in our path but when we were still many miles short of the Jain temple some forty or more cows were standing slam bam in the middle of the road. There they were, solidly and stolidly looking at us, and that we were going to be looking back at them for quite a while became clear when the driver turned off the engine.

Soon, though, he became restless and started to smile and to apologise to us, saying that we probably did not have cow jams in our country.

-Cow jams? No.

-No cow jams?

And I don't know why but in response I found myself coming up with,

-No, we don't, but it doesn't matter at all, having to wait for a bit really doesn't matter. Anyway I like cows. And it's not our world, is it? We share it with all living creatures.

There was a snort and a sharp whisper from my left:

-This wouldn't be Squirrel Killer talking, would it?

****

We halted at a traffic light. Within seconds our car was surrounded with mothers. They were all shoeless. The faces of the mothers were at every window of our car, their children (some of them disabled) in their arms, the mothers' fingernails lightly but insistently tapping the glass for money. Their fingers made money gestures. There was no need for any words or for any translation. You have money, I have not. You know you have lots of money, you know we have none. Look at you and your son being driven like English lords, like English princes, through our country in your expensive clothes and in your expensive car, and then look at us.

Do you not feel ashamed?

Do you not feel guilty?

Do your children and your grandchildren at home in England look like this?

Go on, have a closer look.

Children, those with missing limbs, were held up for me to inspect.

Go on, have a look.

And if I looked the other way, as I wanted to do, if I looked out of Ed's side of the car, I saw a similar sight, a different face, a similar plight. There was no escape from the women and the children, nowhere to hide, nowhere else to look.

While we were still stationary, the driver told us of the devastating effect of the most recent monsoon. The thin tarmac surface of the roads had swelled and buckled, he said, the crops had failed, the mud shelters collapsed, and everything had been made worse by the monsoon.

I am no economist or politician but earlier in the day I had been reading about all this, and about the wider picture after fifty years of Indian independence: about how the abject poor will take any risk because danger is better than poverty, I had read about the effects of inequality on human fertility, how despite all the efforts of governments in recent years 350 million Indians are still below the poverty line – 35% of Indians exist on below £1 a day – and of those 75% live in rural areas such as this.

Only 15% of everything reaches the poor. Why? Because of 'various leakages on the transitional path'. 'Corruption' was the driver's word.

Without even mentioning it to each other Ed and I had avoided talking about all this to any Indian we met, and it was an avoidance not emanating purely from tact or good manners. For how do you say anything beyond the obvious and the banal, and if you have nothing to say beyond the obvious and the banal it is better to say nothing and to give something. Who wants to talk to visitors about the poverty in one's own country? Besides, long before I left England I had got so fed up with the predictably pious remark: 'Oh I couldn't go to India, not with all that poverty everywhere, it would really upset me.' Oh really? Poor you, being so upset. I expect it also upsets the poor Indians.

Also, and this deepens your silence and discomforts you further, you know that you are soon returning to an England in which the obsession – an obsession which particularly afflicts if not characterizes the talented and fortunate young – is to spend every hour of the day making as much money as possible at the expense of all else, and when they are not making money the talented and fortunate ones are talking about it. Some of these young English men and women get bonuses four times as big as the highest annual salary I ever earned.

I am still at a traffic light in India.

The fingernails are still tapping on the car windows.

We are going nowhere.

Each year at Venice Beach in California there is the World Grilled Cheese Eating Championship, where whoever eats the most grilled cheese sandwiches in ten minutes wins $3500. It seems that Don, the current favourite to retain the title, is to eating what Tiger Woods is to golf. 'It's not a competition,' one challenger said, 'it's more a pilgrimage.' I read about that in *The Guardian*, I read about it on the plane over, and saw the photos of the grilled cheese face-stuffing contestants, and the mothers are still tapping, tapping, on our car's windows.

43

Enjoy the good days

Cricket – playing it, coaching it, talking about it, following it – has made me happy, very happy. It has also made me unhappy.

Let's be happy.

Well, at my sort of level, there were any number of last ditch wins by the 3rd XI – the team I coached for over thirty years – when they had played like drains for most of the afternoon and all had long seemed lost, until that special character showed through and they rose to the occasion as one man and snatched the unlikeliest and bravest of victories. And, however you argue it, that *has* to be something to do with the coach.

What else? What about the earliest examples?

Well, on four days in Bristol between July 30th and August 2nd 1952 a small boy saw Tom Graveney make 75, 74, and 113*. Some players 'speak' to you, voice calling to voice across the wide open seas. I was only ten years old but Tom's batting in Bristol on those distant days spoke to me.

Anything else? The Ashes victory of 1953, with Compton and Edrich at the crease when the winning run was hit. The Ashes series of 2005, obviously. And yes, OK, there was that over I bowled one afternoon, I can't be precise about the year but I can be precise about the over, an over in which I bowled six perfectly pitched outswingers, on or just outside off stump, and two batsmen fenced at them and both were caught at first slip. At the other four deliveries they just played and missed.

As a player/a fan/a father the game has lifted me up and, more often than not, it has dashed me down. The truth is that on any given day, in any month, during any season it can do anything to you. It is a lovable game. It is a hateful game. And there is always someone close at hand only too keen to tell you that it is a boring game.

Sometimes, when you are inspired, you feel you can rule the world, you are flying high, you're right up there, no one has ever felt this way before. Everything you do, everything you touch works. Sometimes, when things go wrong, your stomach falls away and your lips are sticking to your gums and you feel small and sick with despair and you want to crawl away and hide.

In July 2003 I saw the sun slowly break through the clouds, and then it hit the small field that mattered most to the Smith family. Early one morning in August 2003, when he was driving to play at Canterbury, the sun suddenly illuminated not one field but the whole hillside: Ed got the call on his mobile from Geoff Miller to say that he was picked to play for England against South Africa in the third test at Trent Bridge. (Tom Graveney's debut was also in the third test and also against South Africa.)

Gillie and I cancelled our holiday to Italy.

Over the years Ed had batted well for spells, and sometimes for weeks at a time – when he was on song a spectator might say to me that there was something special about him – but in the July of 2003 he strung together a sequence of scores that no one, not even his detractors, could ignore.

135, 0, 122, 149, 113, 203, 36, 108, 32.

As always I also saw some of his noughts that season, a season in which he averaged 72.95. If you are a follower seeing failure out there on the pitch is inevitable. I saw the pair he made at Chelmsford. If you don't know what a pair is, it is getting 0 in the first innings and it is getting 0 in the second innings. And they made – as pairs do, as daggers do – two very short and very sharp incisions in my abdomen.

But, hang on, this is the happy chapter, isn't it? Let's enjoy the good moments while we can.

I was at Maidstone in the July of that year for his two

hundreds in the match against Nottinghamshire. One of the many happy aspects of making a hundred (not that I ever made one myself, 87 was my tops) or of watching a hundred being made is that these experiences are not short. Noughts are short. Well, you can of course make a long drawn out nought, a groping nought, one of those extended play and miss play and miss play and miss play and nick oh shit noughts, a nought that goes on for say fifteen minutes, but I can't bear to describe one of those. We're talking here about happy hundreds, and the thing about hundreds is that they do go on. Hundreds can be hours of long and lingering – and justifiably self-congratulatory – pleasure.

Looking back at Maidstone 2003 (Ed scored three hundreds there during that week) seems like watching a dreamlike unedited video in which I am sitting in bright sunshine on the sloping grass under the trees – with four generations of my family – and he is reeling off a series of pulls and straight drives and off drives and cuts and everyone is clapping and saying this lad can play a bit and the ball is rippling to the boundary and the clichés are having an absolute field day.

I'm not sure how I managed it but I even stopped worrying about moving my seat during his second innings against Notts. I broke the rule of a lifetime and stood up.

Madness, I know I know.

With the ice-cream running over the cone and dripping down my fingers I wandered round the boundary in a daze or I stopped for a cup of tea outside the betting tent to watch from a different angle and when I drove into the ground the next day I looked across at the pitch and someone with a familiar stance was out there making it look indecently easy, because the stage was set and he was doing it all over again in the Kent second innings, driving, pulling, cutting and clipping.

That pair in a match against Essex at Chelmsford had given way to two hundreds in a match at The Mote. Perhaps the sun (and the selectors' interest) would now move off his field and luck would desert him and he would slide back to the shadows and suffer another run of low scores. Well, if it happens, it happens. That's the game, son. 'Pour on, I will endure.' Believe me, if King Lear was braced for the worst the gods and his children could do to him, so was I.

A few weeks later a friend rang me up one afternoon.

-Are you watching, Jonathan?

-Watching what?

-Blackpool.

-What about Blackpool?

I did not know that the game between Kent and Lancashire was on Sky and anyway I didn't have Sky and what's more the whole Sky thing made me angry. In fact, most unusually for me, I did not even know that Kent were playing that day. Day and night I was at my desk poring over the proofs of *Night Windows*, my sixth novel, and when I am checking my proofs I go to ground, I batten down the hatches, I become a pedantic teacher with his ruler and his red pen correcting his own homework, and the world of my other obsessions gives me the briefest of breaks.

My friend was having none of this.

-Get to a pub now.

-I'm checking proofs.

-You'll regret it if you don't.

-I can't at the moment. I really can't.

-Look, don't be daft, it may never happen again.

That 'it may never happen again' gave me pause for thought. When things are going well in cricket (or in life?) you can easily slide into the belief that they will continue to do so, assuring yourself that there will be more Maidstones to come, more raisings of the bat at Edgbaston or the Oval or wherever, that these moments are going to be repeated. An unthinking bit of you even starts to believe that things going well is normal. Things going well is not normal. Things going badly is normal. Read some Hardy for God's sake. Read anyone who tells you the truth.

So it is foolish and unforgivable if not fatal – for a player as well as for a fan – to take good fortune and good form for granted. It is so easy to let it all slip through your fingers, to lose it, and 'I've lost it' are among the saddest words any sportsman can say. And who knows the moment when – or indeed if – that good form you are enjoying and taking for granted will ever return?

So get to the pub, Jonathan. Now!

It was a hot day. Even when I'm parched I tend to avoid town pubs, and I particularly avoid them on hot summer afternoons, but I found a smoky seat in the corner of the bar under the telly and, yes, Sky was on (and it looked even hotter up in Blackpool, all the striped deck chairs were out, the knotted hankies were on the heads of the Lancashire faithful and David Lloyd was reminiscing about his youthful indiscretions on the pier), and, glass in hand, I saw Ed pass his highest first class score, which up till then had been 191 against Leicestershire, and then I saw him become the first player to reach a thousand first class runs in the 2003 season, and then, with a four wide of mid on, he notched his first double hundred.

All in one innings against Lancashire.

None of those milestones could ever happen again in any one innings he played. Even though the commentators were talking about a possible test call up for Ed Smith, and even though the camera picked out Geoff Miller sitting there in the Blackpool crowd, in my anxious euphoria I hardly dared to hope.

It would be sad, as I said, if the sun moved off his field on the hillside, if his form deserted him before the selectors made their choice. That has happened to plenty of good players before and since. Sometimes, sod's law, you're up there surfing but by some twist of fate you miss the wave, the wave that really counts, and however hard you try, however much you want it, the opportunity never returns.

44

The bright field

I have seen the sun break through
to illuminate a small field
for a while, and gone my way
and forgotten it. But that was the pearl
of great price, the one field that had
the treasure in it. I realize now
that I must give all that I have
to possess it. Life is not hurrying
on to a receding future, nor hankering after
an imagined past. It is the turning
aside like Moses to the miracle
of the lit bush, to a brightness
that seemed as transitory as your youth
once, but is the eternity that awaits you.

R S Thomas (1913-2000)

45

Trent Bridge

For the Trent Bridge Test, the Third Test against South Africa, we stayed with John Inverarity in his flat in Birmingham. John was then the coach of Warwickshire – indeed the next year he took them to the Championship. Gillie and I travelled up from Birmingham to Nottingham very early each morning, the five mornings of the 14-18th of August, five days that loomed large in our lives.

There was an extra-ness about the drive early that morning on the 14th.

The first morning of a test match.

The first morning of *the* test match.

The first morning of *his* first test match.

We allowed ourselves all the time in the world to get there, but there was a tightness in my chest, a lightness in my head, a heightened sense in the car of a special journey towards the unknown, towards glory or disaster, and then we hit some roadworks on the A this, well, we had to, didn't we, read Thomas Hardy, and then we sat in a long queue and fretted and looked at the map and argued and turned off the A this only to hit even worse delays on the B that, and then what a surprise there was a solid traffic jam all around Trent Bridge. To cap all this we had to collect the tickets Ed had left for us at the gate and there were long queues at the turnstiles (*Enjoy the day!* he had written on the envelope, and his handwriting is as bad as mine) and we were late getting into the ground.

Enjoy the day!

I was very upset to miss seeing him being given his cap by Michael Vaughan. I have a photograph of it in front of me now, Ed in his England cap standing next to Michael Vaughan, but it is not the same thing. Absurdly, I felt we had let him down. We had come all that way, in every sense, only to miss the moment.

Over the years I have missed the moment a number of times. We went to Uxbridge for a Middlesex one dayer against Shane Warne's Hampshire, and as we drove into the car park Ed rang us to ask what we had made of his innings: we had turned up for a 1.30pm start when it began at 11am. He had opened and made a quick 80 odd. Ten years earlier he was playing for Cambridge against Sussex at Hove. I'd checked Ceefax and seen he was going well so I jumped into the car and hurried down the M23 past Gatwick to try to catch a bit of it but – and this is something of a speciality of mine – I couldn't find anywhere to park and I arrived at the ground just too late. It was his second first class hundred. How often have I gone through the gates of a county ground and tried to get a quick glimpse of the scoreboard between the raised seats only to hear the appeal that sends him back to the pavilion?

Even if you're walking along behind the stands and can't see the pitch you can nearly always tell from the nature of the appeal whether or not the batsman will be given out. You can feel the death in your bones. There's nothing phony or dishonest or trying-it-on about the chorus of bowler, wicket-keeper and slips: unsighted successful appeals have that chillingly convincing quality, followed by the shortest of pauses for the umpire's verdict, to be capped by the home crowd's triumphal roar.

Still, we were here in Trent Bridge before the first ball was bowled and having found our seats – West Wing Lower, Row B, seats 25, 26 and 27, I have kept the tickets – my brother David and I went off to buy coffees and scorecards and bottles of Evian. If he won the toss what would Vaughan do? Did I want England to bat first? If we batted first then the first time Ed's feet hit the Trent Bridge turf he would be coming out to bat for England.

What a baptism.

Gulp.

If England fielded first at least he would have a chance to get the feel of the match, to sense the occasion and to run off some of his nerves. My coward's voice also whispered that if England fielded first I myself would feel less pressure. Field first and Gillie and I would quite probably see a whole day of test cricket in which our son (a test cricketer! how I loved that phrase) was playing but was not called upon to bat.

Yes, let's field first.

The coward wins every time.

In the field first scenario I knew I could semi-relax. The doctor's appointment was delayed, the dentist could not fit me in until tomorrow, the surgeon was sorry but there was no bed available. I could eat that sandwich. Yes, it had to come, the knife, the drill, the moment of truth, I knew there was no escaping all that, but not just now, please, not just yet.

And it could always rain.

Look up. No, there was no rain in that sky.

'Good morning, ladies and gentlemen, and welcome to Trent Bridge and the third npower test match between England and South Africa. The teams are as printed on your scorecard. England have won the toss and will bat.'

My stomach went acrobatic. I looked at the scorecard.

M P Vaughan
M E Trescothick
M A Butcher
N Hussain
E T Smith
A J Stewart
A Flintoff
A F Giles
R J Kirtley
S J Harmison
J M Anderson

I looked at the South African bowling attack:

M Ntini
S Pollock
J Kallis
A Hall
P Adams

Hell, some big names there, boy.

****

We had to wait until after tea for Ed to walk down those steps for his (not my) moment of truth. That is a wait from 10.45am, when the first ball was bowled, to 4.15pm. All day I had my bottle of Evian placed on the ground under my seat and I sipped it, only tiny sips, between the overs. I don't know why or how I landed on this latest tactical masterstroke but I decided, if the day was to go well, that I must never sip the water *during* overs. That was my tic that day, and it was a Trent Bridge strategy that I was backing all the way. It could make all the difference. I could make all the difference. I was deadly serious. But, above all, no one must know.

All afternoon, an afternoon of tense lassitude for the Smiths, there was a big stand between Butcher and Hussain. Vaughan and Trescothick were out early, England were two wickets down, but then there was this big stand. A sip of water, another peep at my watch, another glance at the paper, one more clue of the crossword, and a look at the crowd around me. What was it, there was something about them, those spectators. What *was* it? Something didn't add up. In some way I could not put my finger on they were not behaving like most fans at a cricket match.

How long could this waiting, this slow turning of the knife, how long could it go on? Two hours, three hours, four hours. There was no taste to any food I ate. Ed, batting at 5, was padded up for four hours. I could see him on the players' balcony. What was he going through? Wouldn't he be emotionally burnt out before he stood up and put on his helmet and came down the pavilion steps? No, he wouldn't have got this far, he would not have been on the players' balcony in an England shirt if that was the case.

The point is he's not me. He's not me, thank God. Thank God we are different.

A friend who was watching TV in his home rang me to say that I was 'caught on camera' in my pink shirt and looking serious. Apparently, there I was on television in my pink shirt and looking pre-occupied and serious. Well, bugger me, there's a surprise, looking pre-occupied and serious was I, when I could have been dressed as an Elvis look-a-like or done up as a nun with a big tray of lagers and standing up after every boundary and slapping myself and doing the Mexican wave and shouting hey let's lighten up guys it's only a game?

In the course of those long hours of waiting I worked out what it was about the people around me. They were the parents. We had been given tickets in an area reserved for the players' families and friends. Bit by bit I had picked up the atmosphere, the hints, the likenesses and the unusually quiet words. That must be Mr and Mrs Vaughan. And that could well be Mr and Mrs Giles. They could easily be Mr and Mrs Flintoff. Old hands no doubt at all this, all of them.

At the end of the first day's play, with Ed 40 not out – and I watched unblinkingly every ball – we met up in front of the pavilion. He had his England cap on and it looked just right. We all had a hug and a whisper. I can't remember what, if anything, any of us said. It was a blur. Before we left the ground and drove in a daze back to Birmingham a man touched my arm. I turned to face him. I did not know who he was. He looked back towards the players standing outside the pavilion:

-That your lad you were with?

-Yes it is.

-Did well, he did well.

-Thanks, he did.

There are some good spectators in cricket, lots of them in fact – good, ordinary decent fans – and you need to keep reminding yourself of that because as sure as hell there are some horrors who get in your face, hate-filled horrors with hairy arses and beer guts and bad memories who specialize in shouting things like: 'Know what, Smith? You're a muppet!'

****

What do I remember of his innings? Some seconds are clear, and when I am (in Bob Dylan's words) 'clear focused all round', they are shots I can still see and describe, though whole passages of play passed in a swirl of concern.

I remember Adams, the South African spinner, trying to unsettle him with a string of comments, chipping away and chirping at Ed as he walked out to join Nasser Hussain.

I remember Ed smiling and talking to the umpire.

I liked the fact that he smiled and talked to the umpire.

I remember a near run out.

I remember a drive, a cut, and a crisp pull shot for four off Ntini with the new ball.

Smack.

****

Becky, his sister, flew back that night from her holiday in France and hurried (with her baby daughter) up to Nottingham to watch her brother bat on the second morning. We all sat close together as Ed continued on his way. We all nodded at each other as we applauded his fifty. We were all batting, all out there with him.

A fifty on debut.

All those years of playing together in the hall and in the back garden, all those years of bowling at him and fielding for him and willing him on and here we were at Trent Bridge, because all those years had led to this moment.

And when he was caught behind off Kallis for 64 what, if anything, was I thinking? I was thinking:

64 is a score you'd settle for before the game, before any game starts. 64 is fine, any day, any game, let alone in a test match. So we all felt good as we had dinner together in Nottingham that night.

****

In the second innings Ed was out first ball. Hall runs in. It hits Ed on his pads. There is an appeal. Everything about it looked bad. Some LBWs look out even from side on one hundred yards away. My heart stands still. There is a small explosion in my stomach. The umpire's finger goes up. In my gut a small emptiness flares and burns.

LBW Hall, 0.
Fuck.
That is 0 as in nought.
My hopes are blown away.
I tilt.

Swallow hard.
Don't slump.
Deep breath.
Don't buckle.
Put on a brave show.
Retreat into rueful humour.

Odd how the Evian worked in the first innings but not the second.

But no, it's not funny.
I can't stand this.
I hate this game.
I mean it.
I really hate it.

Don't over-dramatise.
No, I'm not, I really really hate it.
Let's end it now.

The nerd sitting behind me in the stand says to his neighbour:
'Yesterday his test average was 64. Today it's 32.'
At the dog-end of the day there is no solace.

46

An Indian alphabet

I haven't stayed in many top hotels, don't be silly, I'm a teacher, but at the top of the top ones I have been inside would come the Taj Mahal Hotel in Mumbai. Walking up the Jazz Age cantilever staircase lifts the spirits, seeing the Gateway to India and the Arabian Sea so huge in the dining room window lifts the spirits, everything, the alabaster and the onyx, the eclectic styles, the fusion of Moorish, Florentine and Oriental, but above all the sense of fun. It feels a fun hotel, and it feels a grand hotel. Having fun and being grand very rarely go together.

So being unable to sleep in such a city and in such a hotel, with a massive moon filling the sky, was not the worst of fates. Nor was it difficult to work out why my mind was buzzing. India and our Rajasthan jaunt were over, and I was flying back home tomorrow: back home to hospital.

We went out to dinner at the Cricket Club of India, which is the equivalent of the MCC in England. It is a place Ed has stayed many times, with the Brabourne Stadium floodlit beneath us, a ground on which he has practised and played. When I got back to my room and accepted that I was not going to drop off to sleep I thought I would try to write a children's book alphabet, one I might read to my granddaughter, Tatiana, when I next saw her in London.

A is for…

In India you can't say A is for apple, Tati, that's far too tame. So how about…

A is for Akbar's mausoleum and the Amber Fort

I lift my binoculars.

B is for bracelets, bats, beggars and bulging buses
Camels, colonnades, cupolas, calligraphy, carpets and cows
– and yes, all right, it's also for cricket
Deserts, dhabawallahs and the white-bellied drongo
E is for elephants, you can't see beyond them
Fatehpur Sikri, flickering eyes, and do peel your fruit
Ghandi, goats, grains of rice, a gauze of mist and a gamut of gurus

(Thomas Hardy says we must look hard and then look harder, so,)

H is for havelis and horns and hoopoes
I am aware of incense and industry and Islam
J is for Jodhpur and Jainism and the pheasant-tailed Jacana
Kites and the Koran and Krishna and the Kama Sutra carvings
Lutyens, the Lake Palace, Lake Pichola, lotus flowers and lattices
And
Mmmm, oh the mmmms there are in India, there are
Mughals and minarets and mirrors and mausoleums (have I said that?) and maharajas and myths and monkeys monkeying around and marble and museums and the monsoon and a massive massive moon in Mumbai
Nehru and the nation
Orchids and oracles
Pavilions, puppet shows, people and people and people all posing the
Question, just how many people are there in India?
Ranakpur, rickshaws, Rahul Dravid, runnels and the rufous treepie
Sharp scents, stoned snakes, silk lined screens, shrines, Sikandra and Vikram Seth
(shoes off and please do not slip on the steps, sir)

Taj Mahal Hotel and textiles and tombs
Udaipur and the Umaid Bhawan and you may find
Vedas and vultures and Vishnu
Where are the women, but with wodka and tonic and so much to see,
Why bother with **X Y** and **Z**ee?

PART TWO

2009

47

Sam in the stadium

-You've never been to the Millennium, have you?
-No.
My brother David was on the phone. He had got a spare ticket for the game against Australia, it's yours if you want it, he said, and he would drive, come on it'll do you good, lunch was laid on, whatever they say it's not the same game on television, lots of old friends would be there, they'd all be at lunch, we always book the same table in the same place, you'll like it, it's only just across the road from the stadium, come on, you won't know yourself, it's always a good day out at Cardiff, all I had to do was say yes.

I'd been to the Arms Park, to the old ground, many times for rugby internationals in the 1950s. That's where, with the mist rising from the River Taff, that's where, on the open terraces, with the wind cutting up from the docks and slicing through your shoulder blades, I was just too young to see the darting Cliff Morgan in his jinking prime and Bleddyn Williams's sidestep and Ken Jones, the flier, on the wing. But it's where I first mingled with the opposing fans, the Irish or the Scots supporters, and we would hail each other and laugh and say look boys it doesn't matter what happens today, eh, as long as we all beat the English.

We used to travel down to Cardiff by bus. It was a red Western Welsh bus and it soon filled up with diesel fumes on the slow grinding climb over the Brecon Beacons, past the reservoirs, and then through Merthyr Tydfil, with the slag heaps coming up on both sides of the road, and Aberfan, where ten years later the landslide would kill 144 people, wiping out Pantglas Junior School, then down the Rhondda Valley, slag heaps as black and shiny as olives and streets tight

201

with miners houses, where Dad was brought up and educated. Porth County was his school. He was very proud of going to Porth County.

Still slightly sick from the fumes we'd step into the big match day atmosphere. Aimless, with time to kill, congregating on corners, we would mill around the streets in macs and duffel coats and, much too young, have an illegal drink. Let's start in the Angel Hotel, boys. The Angel was 'posh'. And after a posh drink, if we were lucky, we would go anywhere they would serve us, somewhere streaming with red, swaggering down any old side street for a few swift ones and a few nifty fags.

For lunch, chips mainly.

-And two pints of Death, please.

-Don't be cheeky, boy, or I won't serve you.

In fact, as with so many football and rugby grounds, the 1950s terraces were dangerously packed. Once you'd found a place to stand on tiptoe, or a barrier to lean on, you couldn't move a muscle let alone an arm or a leg. And after all those frothy beers what chance did you have of fighting your way back out to the Gents? It was a pressing problem, and led to all kinds of things.

> Welshman 1: Got to go.
> Welshman 2: You'll never make it.
> Welshman 1: Got to go. Got to.
> Welshman 2: Don't be daft, piss in that bloke's pocket.
> Welshman 1: Which bloke?
> Welshman 2: The bloke next to you.
> Welshman 1: No, I can't do that.
> Welshman 2: Why not?
> Welshman 1: Well, he'll tell.
> Welshman 2: No, he won't, I've just pissed in yours.

Fifty years later, instead of frothy beer and cigarette smoke it is bottles of Spanish red wine and waiter service. It is strange, and sometimes disturbing, meeting up again with old school friends, people you have hardly seen since you were eighteen. I find everyone has filled out and a few are a bit ponderous on new hips or new knees, and yet somehow everyone is the same. The essence remains. Something in the eyes, some half-landing of the past is in the same place on the stairs: something very hard to define, the spirit of the person, never changes.

In my case, though, the jolt comes straightaway, even as I walk through the door:

-Bloody hell, it's Sam, isn't it?

-What'll you have, Sam?

-Heard you haven't been well, Sammy boy.

-Sam, meet my son.

Only those I grew up with, those I played cricket and rugby with as a boy, still call me Sam. The use of my real name, Jonathan, took over when I left Wales and went to university and that was the end of Sam.

Or, it seems, not.

Hearing my nickname touches and affects me, and at the flick of a switch I am Sam again. In seconds I find myself returning to my youth, to my youthful ways, saying the same sorts of things, using the slightest of Welsh accents, imitating long dead teachers reading the riot act, and nudging the elbows of my old friends as I do so, and someone says it's not very nice that Ed seems to save his big scores for his games against Glamorgan, and I drink too much and tell shamelessly tall stories, they go with the territory, tall stories on match days.

People look at me and expect me to perform and I do, and then I hear myself going on a bit too long or I catch a sceptical look in someone's eye, as if I'm suspect, and I go quiet for a while and look at the beer mats, abstracted and detached, and wonder what on earth this is all about.

About an hour before the kick-off the singing starts. It wells up from every corner of the restaurant, on both floors. *Cwm Rhondda, Calon Lan, Sosban Fach, Mae Hen Wlad fy Nhadau* and a bit of Tom Jones: I was expecting *Delilah* but we got *The Green Green Grass of Home*, with no knickers hurled. They're singing at the bar and they're singing as they go into the Gents, tenor and bass, and they're singing as they come out of the Gents. There must be a hundred men and women in every kind of gear, some in jackets and club ties, some in red Welsh jerseys, some stand up and sway, some have glasses in their hands as they sing, there are townies and farmers, women in Welsh skirts, men with tattoos and leathers, red T-shirts, Welsh scarves, every kind of person in every manner of dress. And one of the waitresses has dangerously long legs.

They sing all the hymns and all the songs you would expect from a warming up Welsh crowd, and they do not suffer from shyness. I'm a lousy singer and my Welsh is worse so instead of joining in I listen and watch.

You won't know yourself.

I wonder if J P R Williams is in Cardiff.

Bound to be.

Twenty minutes before the kick-off we – is it we or is it they? – it's we, we all drain our creamy Irish coffees and the expresso hisses as we pass the bar and we smack our lips and empty out on to the street, we're territorial now, and we surge across to the stadium to do battle.

-Right, boys. *Delilah.*

The thing is, I'm not sure I really belong on the streets of Cardiff. In truth I don't think I ever did, but part of me is swept up in the Millennium moment, it's not phoney, and I am glad to be there and proud to be following the boys.

48

Influences

For over two years I couldn't write. It wasn't that I threw in the towel or anything dramatic like that. It wasn't as if I was pathetic. God no. Almost from the moment I was coming round in the recovery room, with the nurse's face swimming in and out of focus, I was talking to myself in the sternest possible way about picking up my pencil and facing the blank page and getting back down to it. Lying there in the hospital ward with tubes coming out of everywhere I told myself that if I got well I would be so grateful to be alive that I would not only write something every single day but I would also, and most importantly, stop worrying about all the stupid things I couldn't change. Like cricket. Cricket is a game. Sport is not life and death. Right. Got that one out of the way. At last.

And when I got home I was as good as my word: I did scribble down the odd sentence and I did make a few starts and when I re-read it and felt myself going into a nose-dive I did give myself regular lectures on guts, on how gutsy people always kept going, on how gutsy people always kept slugging it out, absolutely I did, but the fact was I couldn't really *write*. Had some part of me died? Had the surgeon cut more parts out of me than I was told? There were a few worrying signs. The electricity in my hands was not there, the hunting energy, the girl's glance, the tension, the quarry, the scent, the chase, all the stuff that goes to make the story and the book – all that seemed to have gone. It felt a libidinous loss. Should I hang up my boots? Was it time to hold up my hands and call it a day?

But somehow or other the day out at Cardiff with my brother stirred me up, and as I was going home after the match a voice in my head kept saying: 'Keep close to the ground, keep close to what moves you, keep close to what you know.' The voice was Larkin's.

I am sitting in my wooden hut in my garden with a pencil in my hand. It is now February 2009 and I am feeling OK. No, I am feeling more than OK: I am feeling happy (or about as happy as I ever get) because I am a few pages into a new radio play for the BBC. They've commissioned it. In fact they've commissioned more than one.

Even more than that, the icing on the cake, outside the kitchen window six goldfinches are feasting, I can see them from here. Sometimes we get eight, ten's a field day: a charm of goldfinches, all flighty and bouncy and dancing, red and yellow and black and white, they're the most beautiful little birds, they really are, and they've been lured in to our garden by the niger seeds we put out. They drop in every morning.

Yesterday I also saw a pair of long-tailed tits.

And a nuthatch. A sleek nuthatch.

In my neighbour's garden there is a slowly diminishing snowman, and my car windows are still frozen white, but with the heater on this oaken hut warms up in no time. If I need a rest, as I sometimes do after a spell of concentrated work, I've got a chaise longue up against one wall. The chaise longue, a modern job, is on long loan from Ed, and if I lie down I can see a new postcard pinned up on a beam above my head. I've taken to sending encouraging messages to myself. This one comes from David Simon, who created *The Wire*, and it reads: 'Fuck the average viewer.' On the other wall is one from Chekhov. 'Everything I read now seems not short enough.'

The squirrels are, of course, still completely out of control. Nothing new there.

Their latest game is to scamper all over the roof of my hut as soon as they spot I am at my desk. For all its lightness this scampering breaks my concentration and irritates me to hell and back, and for old times' sake – to show that even in these post-op days I haven't entirely given up on violence – I make the occasional foray, hoping by my skirmish to spread a little ruin and desolation in the south-east, but they just do a sidestep and a leaping gear change, like a Welsh fly half playing with the opposition, like Barry John or Phil Bennett, and they are off along a swaying apple tree branch, then leap leap bounce bounce, and they're over the wall to safety.

Once I've picked up my pencil again and have settled down to a sentence, they sneak back. Basically they're having a laugh. Basically they are taking the piss. Squirrels, as far as I can see, are rats with bushy tails.

Still, squirrels or no squirrels, I've sharpened my 3B pencils, all ten of them, and I'm back on the case.

****

A friend rang to say that Ed was on the radio this morning. I missed it. At the end of January his third book, *What Sport Tells Us About Life*, came out in paperback, so the more exposure he gets, the more interviews he has the merrier. That's what all writers and all publishers crave, isn't it, a bit of author visibility, and the wave might be with him because in recent days cricket has been hogging the headlines, what with the Pietersen and Moores captain/coach muddle and then the Indian Premier League auctions – big egos and big bucks – not to mention the terrorist attack on the Sri Lankan cricketers in Lahore.

I don't feel nervous hearing Ed on the *Today* programme or watching him on *Newsnight*. It's not like cricket. It's nothing like being at the ground as he comes down the pavilion steps because this time he can't be dismissed for 0, can he? I mean, John Humphrys and Jeremy Paxman may know how to fire in their own beamers and bouncers, they may think they're the most feared attack in the world, the broadcasting equivalents of Michael Holding and Malcolm Marshall at Sabina Park, but if Ed plays a bad intellectual shot or misses a yorker in the argument he has plenty of time to recover. The interviewers, all cocked eyebrows, can say oh come off it, they can snarl and growl all they like, but he's still out there on the media pitch, and still batting. He hasn't been sent back to the dressing room cursing himself every step of the way, he isn't on the humiliatingly slow return to the pavilion, unpeeling his gloves, taking off his helmet, with the crowd eloquent in their silent stony criticism. (How does the line go? 'Remember, we're all in this alone.')

Talking about sport on the media, I have to say, strikes me as dead easy. Writing about it is not dead easy but it is not all that difficult either. It is playing sport consistently well at a high level which brings the problems.

With his third book out in the shops people are increasingly asking me whether I have influenced Ed as a writer, and, if so, in what ways. It's impossible to answer, it really is, any more than I could measure the shaping input I have had from my daughter on the early drafts of my novels and plays.

But it goes much wider than my children: I have been massively influenced by my friends, by small asides they make, not to mention the writers I most admire, some of whose poems and extracts are woven into this book. When tributaries run into rivers, you cannot separate the water even a few yards down stream.

We have influenced each other, Ed and I, that much is obvious. If you talk as we do, if you share ideas and test your perceptions and challenge each other as we have, I wouldn't know how to establish where it all begins or ends. We may discuss our individual plans and projects in some detail, but we may or may not allow each other to read our opening chapters. We may explain and defend, and explain and defend all over again, but then we try to hold on to the individual impulse and the individual voice. There's only so far you can go with all that sharing. When you write you're not in a choir, you're a soloist.

Sometimes I feel altogether too vulnerable for a high level of conceptual engagement. This is especially so if I am fumbling my way into something new. Ed is a clear thinker and in my fumbling moods the one thing I do not want is clear thinking. I often have no sense of the direction in which I am heading, but I do know that I must not force it because if I force it there's a chance I will lose the scent, a chance I will lose the sharp stink of fox that Ted Hughes captures.

So I allow my feet to be drawn on and trust myself to find a path.

At this stage of any project I'd rather be left well alone, left to my own devices. It is almost as if I am ill, as if I am sickening for something nasty. I am trying to steal up on things at an angle, I know that much, but I don't yet know exactly what. It's as if I am stealing up on goals which I can't clearly see, almost pretending that they're not there, staking out the territory, stalking an elusive and unnamed prey, testing the water, trying the side door, nosing a story rather than taking it head on. My rare creative surges, such as they are, stem more from unfocused feeling than from conscious thought.

I was into my mid thirties when I started to write. Well, I had published a critical edition of Shakespeare's *King Lear* in my late twenties, but I was 33 when I nervously handed in my first novel, *Wilfred and Eileen*, which I think of as my first proper book. At twenty one Ed was already reviewing fiction for the *Sunday Telegraph*. I can remember the book he was sent for his first review, and how lucky he was to be offered it. It was *The Whereabouts of Aeneas McNulty* by Sebastian Barry, a lyrical novel of an innocent who was buffeted by history.

Four years later Ed came up with a book of his own, *Playing Hard Ball*, a two-sided portrait of cricket and baseball. And he has been writing ever since. That's what writers have to do, keep writing. If you're a writer you have to keep getting your bat on it. You must take guard and look around the field without being intimidated by the opposition. If you raise your head above the parapet, if you decide you want to play in the first place, there's no point complaining that you're outnumbered. You *are* outnumbered and you always will be. If you're not sure about that, go into a bookshop and look around. You chose the life. So don't worry who your competitors are or what they might be up to. All that does is drain away your energy. Much better to focus on what you are trying to achieve.

In close-up shots on television, as the bowler is running in, the camera often picks up the batsman saying (or silently mouthing) to himself: 'Watch the ball, watch the ball.' And he's right, I think, to be saying that. As a mantra, as self-instruction, it is simple and sensible advice. The first time he makes clean contact, the first time he feels his bat hit (or *middle*) the ball, it feels good and the relief is palpable, allowing the jumping nerves to settle just a fraction, helping the heart to hammer a little less hard.

You've written down the first word and that's a start, so well done. It's not yet an opening sentence – let alone a good opening sentence – but you've put down a marker, you're off the mark, and now you must run the singles, rotate the strike, run another single, build a partnership with the reader, in the hope that eventually, in the fullness of time, the reader will be your accomplice.

Between the overs you may be tempted to go for a mid-pitch chat and to punch gloves with the reader. If you are tempted to punch gloves make sure you do so modestly not cockily, because many readers do not like you to presume an unearned intimacy. Readers do not want to be taken for granted. They like a little decorum. So keep your head down, build up the paragraphs, take it one ball at a time, don't think of a half century, don't think of a hundred, and above all don't dream of a standing ovation from a packed test match crowd with your bat held triumphantly aloft, that is dangerous, don't do it, do not do it, think a sentence at a time, think ten runs at a time, a page a day would be a book a year, not that you should necessarily be aiming for that, too many writers write too much as it is, so don't get greedy, turn the tens into twenties and the twenties into fifties, and the chapters will grow one by one and may eventually, even surprisingly, turn into a book.

Unless you are a genius, or exceptionally lucky, a great deal will go wrong. There will be plays and misses and big lunges and unproductive spells and air-shots and mis-hits and rushes of blood and false dawns and, in all probability, only a full waste paper basket as your companion.

With a lot of good fortune, if everything goes your way, you might make a hundred, or at least turn in a decent performance. Every dog has his day. But even the best writers don't score hundreds every time, though their blurb writers and their publicists love to suggest that they do.

So, what do I say to myself?

I say to myself, however well you do, you cannot make runs if you are not at the crease. You cannot score runs in the practice nets, where extravagant shots tend to result in fantasy boundaries and fantasy triumphs – but carry the risk of dangerous self delusion. Equally, you cannot write by talking about writing.

So… stop talking and sit down.

Pick up your pencil.

Or turn on your computer.

And start.

As you cannot improve a first draft that you have not yet written, I would urge you – particularly in these early stages – to be kind to yourself. It is all too easy to give yourself a hard time and to cross out the first thing you write. All that critical editing and necessary re-writing is a long way off, and the 'first sentence' in your published book may well have been your fifteenth attempt at it. But for the moment, as you get into your stride, put your critical mind on hold.

In other words, do not – as I tend to do – allow your heavy handed judgemental self to thud up the steps into the pulpit and, from capacious sleeves, point the finger accusingly at your creative self sitting in the pews below, his pride hurting, feeling small, another failed writer who dared to court the muse.

Much better to keep your head down.

Watch the ball.

Don't get ahead of yourself.

Watch the ball.

(And re-reading the last couple of pages it is all too clear that I have never really left the classroom.)

So I follow Ed's career in the world of sport, and he follows me into world of writing. Except that his cricket career is finished. He's hung up his boots. A few months ago he collected his kit from his corner of the dressing room at Lord's, wheeled his *coffin* to the door – how typical of cricket to use that term for a kit bag – and looked around for the last time. Or I imagine he did.

There is no doubt at all that in the widest sense I will remain a follower and a fan until the day I die, but that particular part, the following Ed bit, is over.

49

The Loving Game

Before their big fights, if you believe Norman Mailer, boxers 'begin to have inner lives like Hemingway or Dostoyevski, Tolstoy or Faulkner, Joyce or Melville'. No, you're absolutely right, I don't believe a word of it either. Put it this way, how many boxers do you know who write poems? Come to that, how many poets do you know who are into boxing?

Well, here's one. Vernon Scannell. *The Loving Game* is a poem by a semi-professional middleweight boxer who really could write. As a fighter he won titles at school and at university and for a while he worked in a fairground boxing-booth. Not only that, he was also a schoolteacher who wrote novels and loved jazz and friendly women and London pubs.

Born John Vernon Bain, he changed his name to Vernon Scannell while he was on the run from the army. He was a man who described himself as 'torn apart between the irreconcilable passions of literature and sport'. One of us, then.

A quarter of a century ago
I hung the gloves up, knew I'd had enough
Of taking it and trying to dish it out,
Foxing them or slugging it toe-to-toe;
Keen youngsters made the going a bit too rough;
The time had come to have my final bout.

I didn't run to fat though, kept in shape,
And seriously took up the loving game,
Grew moony, sighed, and even tried to sing,
Looked pretty snappy in my forty-drape.
I lost more than I won, earned little fame,
Was hurt much worse than in the other ring.

Vernon Scannell (1922-2007)

50

Lord's, 12th June 2008

The moment it happened, my daughter Becky and I – possibly the two most superstitious people still on the planet – were sitting next to each other in the Long Room at Lord's. I very rarely go into the Long Room to watch the cricket, high and handsome though it is, because I don't feel at ease in the hush, and with the sightscreens so wide I often find it difficult to find a seat with an unhampered view of the playing area, but for some reason that is where Becky and I were perched on that June evening.

That same afternoon I had returned to hospital for a check up: always a bit of a moment, that, waiting to see which way the umpire goes. What's his decision? What's the verdict? Out? Not out? Close call? Or is he giving me the benefit of the doubt? In fact the test results were encouraging but I didn't bring them up in the Long Room. Why risk a reversal in fortune by saying everything is going well so far? Much better to sit tight, don't move your seat, stay where you are, and hope the partnership between you and life continues.

Out in the middle, in front of 20,000 fans, a huge crowd for any county cricket match, Middlesex were playing Essex in an evening 20/20 fixture. It was the second game of the 20/20 season. Middlesex had won their first 20/20 contest down at the Rose Bowl against a strong Hampshire side (and Kevin Pietersen) and were well on their way to another victory when Ed broke his ankle.

Essex had batted first and were all out for 115, with the Middlesex bowlers and fielders always on top. In fact, after a patchy start to their summer, by 12th June Middlesex were on a bit of a roll. They were second in their division of the championship. They were winning their fifth match on the trot, a sequence including beating Essex in the four day game by an innings the week before, when Ed turned for a second run at the bowler's end and went down in a heap.

Throughout his career he had always, fingers crossed, been fortunate with his fitness. Perhaps he was lucky to escape the major injuries that shorten so many sporting lives, and only a fool rules out the importance of luck. Apart from a finger broken in 1998 when he was batting against the South Africans at Cambridge he had played many seasons without missing a game of any kind. For seven years he had been picked for every championship match at Kent and Middlesex. But this time I knew in my bones that it was bad.

-He's OK, isn't he, Dad?

-Doesn't look good.

-No, he's going to be all right.

-Not sure.

He eventually got to his feet and stayed at the crease, with Andrew Strauss (who was already out) coming on from the pavilion, padded up and ready to run for him. Ed could hardly take his stance. Once or twice I thought he was going to keel over as he shaped to play a stroke, but that didn't stop Pettini, the Essex skipper, questioning the umpire over whether Ed really needed a runner.

Ah, the spirit of cricket!

His last shot in that game at Lord's or in any game – as it proved to be his last scoring stroke in professional cricket – was a four to the Mound Stand off Danish Kaneria, the Pakistani spinner. A few minutes later he was out.

E T Smith c Chambers b Kaneria 33

Becky and I watched him hobble slowly off the field with Strauss, and then up the steps into the pavilion and past us in the Long Room and past the portraits and the glass display cabinets and out of the door at the far end and up to the home dressing room. He didn't see us or know we were there.

Middlesex went on to win the game by seven wickets, and indeed, a few weeks later, to win the 20/20 finals at The Rose Bowl. It was their first trophy in fifteen years.

Not long after his injury, I met up with Ed in London and saw his ankle for the first time. It had swollen to twice its normal size, while his leg was black and yellow up to the knee. An X ray later showed that his fibula was in two pieces.

****

With his ankle still not right, on 24th November 2008 he retired at 31 from the first class game.

51

In a garden in Athens

It isn't easy coming to terms with the end of something which has meant so much, something which had absorbed him and his family for so long, something which perhaps came to mean almost too much. On his side it had been a life fully lived and, on my side, a life vicariously lived.

I suppose I could play it all down. I could say what does it matter, what's all the fuss about, grow up, it's just a game, just a game with a ball and a piece of wood for God's sake, and I could pretend that we all took it in our stride, but then what would be the point of my writing this book? If you don't understand what playing at the top level is like, or accept the demands such a life makes, if you don't know about fathers and sons and sport, you may find it hard to grasp how deeply all this goes for those who perform and for those who follow, especially if it is in the family.

Ed had a bat in his hand from the age of two. Now, for the first time in his life, he would not. If something has been that big, it leaves a big hole.

There were difficult days in the summer of 2008. But after it was all over I began to feel, I have to admit, a growing sense of relief. And in the relief there was also an undercurrent of guilt at my own response. Because now he had retired from cricket I could turn up to a match and behave like a normal human being, like a normal fan. If he was not playing I could say any one of the following:

'Yes, I will have a drink.'
'What's the score?'
'Hey, it's great to be here.'
'Doesn't the ground look a picture today!'
'What a catch!'

And – without building too much expectation or tempting fate – I could also nod like a wise old bird and say of someone else's son:

'Tell you what, this bloke can play a bit.'

When you're not personally involved you can be sociable and say all the sociable stuff and you can even mean it. When your son isn't out there on the pitch you can be balanced and even-handed in your praise, treating friend and foe alike. You can be mature and grown up. When one of your family is batting or bowling, though, or circling under a high catch a few feet in from the boundary rope, with 20,000 watching, your stomach can rise swiftly to your gorge or go into a long free-fall. Ask any parent.

His retirement meant, then, that I wouldn't be churned up and flickering with hope every day of every summer. I would no longer be on the edge of my seat at the ground or, even worse, in thrall to Ceefax and to cricinfo. The English cricket season lasts a full six months, from early April to late September, from chill spring till the last feel of the sun, and they're stretching it out all the time. That is half of every year, more than half if you add a pre-season tour, and even longer if you play overseas in the winter. And if you're the captain of the club, it is twelve months a year full on. Not only would he never again have to face success or failure on the field of play, I, too, would be off the rack. The shackles would be gone. The madness would loosen its grip on me.

I am not proud of that admission, it's not good, I know my reaction is out of all proportion, but it is the truth.

****

So, given all this, is sport good for you?

Good for your character, that is?

I have often wondered about that, and I would answer it differently on different days, led by my changing moods or reacting to my latest experience, but as a teacher and a father and a follower I am sure of one thing: sport, for better or worse, does reveal your character. And that goes for the fans in the stands and the fathers on the touchline as well as the players on the pitch.

As I finish this last chapter I also ask myself if how much I cared made it all the more difficult for Ed as a player. Would it have been more helpful if I had quietly tuned out, stayed away, written more and watched less, not had the long phone calls, and kept a fatherly eye on him from an adult distance? Even worse, did the private intensity of my involvement in his cricketing career handicap him in some way?

I've never put that to him straight and he would deny any of the implications, I know he would, but the question still nags and is unlikely to go away.

More than that, though – much more than that – I feel gratitude for all the game has given him, for the highs, obviously for the highs, but more for all he's been through, all we've been through with him, all the knocks he has taken, and also some (I hope permissible) pride in what he has achieved. He made nearly 13,000 runs, including 34 hundreds, and he averaged just under 42. He played for Cambridge, his university, he played for Kent, his home county, he captained Middlesex, and he was picked for England.

And sometimes I was there.

And when I wasn't I was.

****

I was sitting in a garden in Athens on the day after the funeral of my oldest friend, Roger Parsons – Roger had died of cancer – when my mobile went. I knew who it was. No one else rings me on my mobile. Ed had delayed making the call with his news in case it upset us. We chatted for a bit, and he asked me how things were in Athens, how Gillie and I were, how Roger's wife and his daughters were coping, and then he told me that the cricket was all over, but that we weren't to worry about anything on his account, that he was fine.

Now he could concentrate on his writing.

And so could I.

All You Who Sleep Tonight

All you who sleep tonight,
Far from the ones you love,
No hand to left or right
And emptiness above –

Know that you aren't alone
The whole world shares your tears –
Some for two nights or one,
And some for all their years.

Vikram Seth (1952-)